# FAITH
# AND
# PHILOSOPHY

## David Patterson

UNIVERSITY
PRESS OF
AMERICA

Copyright © 1982 by
**University Press of America,Inc.™**
P.O. Box 19101, Washington, D.C. 20036

Library of Congress Cataloging in Publication Data

Patterson, David.
    Faith and philosophy.

    Includes index.
    1. Philosophy and religion--Addresses, essays,
lectures.  2. Faith--Addresses, essays, lectures.
I. Title.
BL51.P317  1982        200'.1        81-43469
ISBN 0-8191-2651-9

To my wife and daughter

# ACKNOWLEDGEMENTS

I would like to extend my sincere thanks to Madame Nathalie Baranoff for allowing me to cite passages from Lev Shestov's Na vesakh Iova (Paris: La société nouvelle d'Editions Franco-Slaves, 1929) and from Shestov's Umozrenie i otkrovenie (Paris: YMCA Press, 1964).

My thanks also to Princeton University Press for allowing me to quote from Soren Kierkegaard, Fear and Trembling, tr. Walter Lowrie, Copyright 1941 © 1969 by Princeton University Press, selected passages, pp. 41-84, reprinted by permission of Princeton University Press.

Portions of Essay I originally appeared under the title of "Abraham and Kierkegaard: A New Approach to the Father of Faith" in the Journal of Religious Studies, 8 (Spring 1980), 8-19, whom I thank for permission to reprint.

Portions of Essay II originally appeared under the title of "Shestov's Second Dimension: In Job's Balances" in the Slavic and East European Journal, 22 (1978), 141-151, to whom I give my grateful acknowledgement.

Portions of Essay III originally appeared under the title of "The Unity of Existential Philosophy and Literature as Revealed by Shestov's Approach to Dostoevsky" in Studies in Soviet Thought, 19 (1979), 219-231, Copyright © 1979 by D. Reidel Publishing Company, Dordrecht, Holland, to whom I extend my grateful acknowledgement for permission to reprint.

Portions of Essay IV originally appeared under the title of "The Movement of Faith as Revealed in Tolstoy's Confession" in the Harvard Theological Review, 71:3-4 (1978), 227-243, Copyright 1978 by the President and Fellows of Harvard College, to whom I am grateful for permission to reprint.

# TABLE OF CONTENTS

# PREFACE

There are times in perhaps each of our lives when
the light goes out and the groundwork crumbles. Ham-
let's question haunts us (oh do not ask, "What is it?"),
and we seem to be stranded somewhere else, unable to
get back to ourselves. Nothing makes sense, the handrails elude us; all we have left is passion and outcry.

The essays in this book touch on the metaphysics
of outcry that may be involved in the self-to-self,
self-to-other and self-to-world relationships which
shape our lives. They are for anyone who has ever loved
or laughed, wept or cursed. The faith and philosophy
dealt with here come largely from the Western tradition,
but the last essay should bring out a link or two between East and West. Indeed, the twain seem to meet
more and more often as the world continues to shrink.
Although the essays have been written as independent
entities, there are certain ties that bind them; the
echoes of one found in another may shed light one both.
Unless otherwise indicated, all translations are my own.

In committing these thoughts to paper, I do not
presume to explain or enlighten. In the words of Wiesel,
I write more to understand than to be understood.

# INTRODUCTORY ESSAY

## FAITH AND PHILOSOPHY

Faith and philosophy: two big words for thought to tackle, two words often in conflict, for the ways of one are not the ways of the other. They speak different languages, raise different questions, embrace different concerns. Rarely do the names associated with faith turn up among the names of the great philosophers. Seldom do the two find their roots planted in the same soil.

Faith arises when it has no business being there. It comes suddenly, when the chain of cause and effect is broken, when the balances go awry and the world turns to nothing. It lives on a promise that cannot be kept and sets out for a place that cannot be found. The truths of the eyes are left behind; the handrails and horizons of the impossible dissolve. Faith buries all sense and sensibility and rolls away every sepulcher's stone.

Philosophy is born in the Fall, when the craving for knowledge overwhelms the blindness of faith. It arises when Thales falls into a well while walking along gazing at the heavens and then resolves never to take a step unless he is sure of the ground beneath his feet. It emerges again when Philo teaches Thomas to take nothing on faith and to accept only what his eyes can see. And again it appears when Descartes doubts even the evidence of the eyes yet clings to the natural light of the clear and distinct.

When faith encounters philosophy there is a collision between Paul's dictum that whatever is not of faith is sin and the Socratic assertion that ignorance is sin, between the storm of passion and the calm of reason, between the abyss and the firm ground. Philosophy cannot sustain such a collision without going unchanged. It must either turn away from faith or undergo such a transformation that we may hesitate to call it philosophy. In this essay I shall examine the encounter between faith and philosophy and consider what happens to philosophy in the aftermath.

## 1

According to Hasidic legend, Rebbe Hersh, son of

1

the Baal Shem Tov, once had a dream in which his dead
father appeared to him. He took the opportunity to
question his father about the nature of faith, asking,
"How shall I serve God? How shall I find the path that
leads to Him?" His father replied by ascending the
heights of a great summit and casting himself into the
abyss, shouting, "Like this, my son!" Then the Baal
Shem again came forth and rose up in a mountain of fire
that exploded in a thousand flaming fragments, crying,
"And like this!"[1]

Here we see the images of Abraham and Elijah gathered together: from the summit of Moriah Abraham cast
himself into the deep as he raised the knife over Isaac,
and at Bethel Elijah was snatched from the side of
Elisha as he rose into the heavens in a whirlwind of
fire. Such are the elements of faith—the fire and the
whirlwind of deep calling to deep. Such is the substance of Abraham, Elijah and every human being. For
"man is made of faith," as it is written in the Gita.
"As his faith is so he is."[2]

Whatever faith I have, that I am. Faith means I am.
Whenever we move in faith it is I Am who moves us. The
I Am arises not from the cogito but from the flames of
passion: faith is a passion. But it is not the passion
of melodrama, of flailing arms and gnashing teeth. As
he walked beside his father on the way to Moriah, Isaac
discerned nothing in his father's gait that might have
betrayed the old man's passion. In the words of
Kierkegaard,

> To be able to fall down in such a way
> that the same second it looks as if one
> were standing and walking, to transform
> the leap of life into a walk, absolutely
> to express the sublime in the pedestrian
> —that only the knight of faith can do.[3]

This is how faith pronounces I Am—not in the confusion of tongues but in the silent expression of the
sublime in the pedestrian. "The raging revelations upon
which religions are founded," writes Buber, "are essen-
tially the same as the quiet ones that are given everywhere and at all times."[4] One of the most striking elements in the story of the Binding of Isaac is the silence of Abraham throughout the trial. Kierkegaard was
the first to take note of this, the first to understand
that Abraham cannot speak, for to state his case would

be to lose his case. As soon as he opens his mouth, he must speak as the world speaks, the world in which he was a man reputed for his justice. But on the road to Moriah all sense of justice is completely undone; Abraham is justified by faith alone. This is what makes his silence resound through the ages. For faith, silence is word, word silence.

Silently Abraham walks. The silence calls him forth. The I Am of faith is not an announcement but a beckoning. Deep calls to deep. It is only by saying, "Here I am," that Abraham is called forth, for "Here I am" means "That Thou art." The ehyeh asher ehyey (I Am That I Am) of Exodus goes with the tat tvam asi (That Thou Art) of the Upanishads. This is how we are to understand Buber's assertion that the I finds its presence only by saying Thou; becoming I, I say Thou.5 Saying, "Here I am," I say, "That Thou art."

If faith is relegated to the Single One, it brings the single I before the single Thou. The single presence born of faith is the presence of two—Abraham and Isaac, Jacob and the Angel, Elijah and Elisha, Brahman and Atman. Abraham's ability to walk with God lies in his ability to walk with Isaac; his love for God is precisely his love for Isaac. It is important not to read into this a father/son or master/slave principle. If there is a "principle" at work here it is the person/person principle, the idea that there is no relation between man and man that is not a relation between man and God. Thus when faith is at the heart of the matter, there is no relationship between God above and man below. The God above is either a demon or an illusion. The relation, rather, is between God and man alongside each other, and God and man come together when man and man come together. The Hebrew letter yud is a mere dot, but when two of these letters are written together, side by side, they signify the name of God; written one above the other, they indicate an interruption.6

Faith dwells neither in God nor in man but in between, in the relation, where the spirit dwells. To say that faith is a passion is to say that faith is spirit, more like the air we breathe than the blood that flows in our veins. Faith is the risk more daring by a breath, the movement beyond all clamoring for security. The movement of faith is a movement into the in-between, into the open, where the I offers all to the Thou, all

and for nothing. Just as when Abraham departed from the
firm ground of family and home, faith leaves behind all
coordinate systems, all points of reference, everything
from which we normally draw the strength to live: the
stars go out, the sun turns to darkness, and the moon
turns to blood.

Such is the madness of faith. It is the madness of
Job when he declares, "Though after my skin worms destroy this body, yet in my flesh shall I see God: whom
I shall see for myself, . . . I and not another; though
my reins be consumed within me" (Job 19:26-27). Reality
and illusion exchange places. Eyes that no longer exist
—the eyes of Job and not another—will see the God who
cannot be seen. A child consigned to death—the child
Isaac—is to be the seed of generations. Moses, the
stutterer, becomes the spokesman for Israel. And
Abraham sets out for the Promised Land with no idea of
where he is going. What could be more outrageous, more
offensive, more ridiculous?

Dostoevsky's Grand Inquisitor understood the madness and outrage of faith only too well. He knew that
we who live by bread alone cannot survive unless the
stones are turned to bread; that since we believe only
what our eyes behold, our counterfeit faith requires
miracles to sustain itself; and that we long to lay our
freedom at the feet of authority because the dizzying
groundlessness of freedom is too much for our frail
souls to bear. "I emerge alone and in anguish," writes
Sartre, "in the face of the unique and primary project
which constitutes my being. All the barriers, all the
guard rails collapse, annihilated by the consciousness
of my freedom."[7] This is what haunts the Grand Inquisitor; this is the impetus behind his cause. The Grand
Inquisitor is a man shaped by his longing for the
greatest happiness of the greatest number: the essence
of his mission is to deliver humankind from the agonies
of freedom. As he sees it, we cannot bear the burden of
freedom because we cannot make the movement of faith.

The movement of faith is the movement of freedom;
the more faith, the more freedom. Though freedom treads
no ground, faith keeps it from falling, "transforming
the leap of life into a walk." To be free is to embark
upon the dangerous perhaps, to leap into the abyss, to
explode into a mountain of fire. For "freedom is fire,"
as Norman O. Brown has declared.[8] And fire is passion.

Another word for the fire and passion of faith is love. If faith goes with redemption, it is love that so consigns it. Unlike feelings that reside within, love, like the spirit, arises between, in the relation of an I to a Thou. Only through love can an I say Thou with the whole of its being. Indeed, this is precisely what makes it whole; through love I Am and That Thou Art are gathered together. Faith offers all, all and for nothing, because faith is made of love. If the offering should be made in order to avoid judgement or to gain entry into the kingdom, then the offering is reduced to a kind of bargaining and the temple turned over to the merchants. In short, love and the faith that engenders it are lost.

It must be noted, again, that the love which goes with faith is not the love of man below for God above. Rather, it is man's love for God revealed in his love for a fellow human being. The two great commandments— to love God and to love your neighbor—are of a piece; there is no love for one without love for the other. Jesus made the two commandments into a single request: that we love one another as he loves us. This means that we face the same trial of faith that was upon Abraham: the sacrifice of what we love with all our heart, all our mind, all our soul. Perhaps Feuerbach can help to make this clear:

> God is love, but because of his love, of the predicate, it is that he renounced his Godhead; thus love is a higher power and truth than deity. Love conquers God. . . . Who then is our Saviour and Redeemer? God or Love? Love; for God as God has not saved us, but Love, which transcends the difference between the divine and human personality. As God has renounced himself out of love, so we, out of love, should renounce God; for if we do not sacrifice God to love, we sacrifice love to God, and, in spite of the predicate of love, we have the God—the evil being—of religious fanaticism.[9]

God is indeed a consuming fire, as it is written (Deuteronomy 4:24), a fire by which He is Himself consumed. Here lies the fear and trembling of Moriah, the dread and mystery of Golgotha—in short, the heart and substance of faith.

From what has been said it should not be difficult to see why philosophy cast in the mold of speculative thought may have some trouble in laying its hands on faith. Who can fail to be struck by the contrast between Abraham, who set out without knowing where he was going, and Thales, who insisted on knowing beforehand where his foot would fall? Such is the red and the black of the father of faith opposite the father of speculative philosophy. Shestov expresses it quite eloquently in this image from Athens and Jerusalem:

> For the prophets and apostles, faith is
> the source of life; for the philosophers
> of the Middle Ages enlightened by the
> Greeks, it is the source of knowledge
> and understanding. How can one fail to
> recall the two trees God planted in the
> Garden of Eden at the time of the crea-
> tion?10

When the Fruit is eaten, the eyes of speculative philosophy are opened. Speculative philosophy—a philosophy which takes reason to be the highest court in determinations of truth, philosophy which identifies reality with rationality, philosophy rooted in the principle of contradiction—is a philosophy of the eyes. It is a philosophy which takes no risks,which always looks before it leaps, and which, therefore, never makes the decisive leap. Thales insisted on seeing the firm ground, watching his every step. Philo, the Hellenistic Jew of Alexandria, set out to correct the Scriptures by changing the voice of God into a vision of God. Descartes operated according to the natural light, basking in what he took to be clear and distinct. And Husserl declared that "if phenomena have no nature, they still have an essence, which can be grasped and adequately determined in an immediate seeing."11 All were sun worshipers, transfixed by the Apollonian illusion; all shunned the blotting out of the light, the madness, that characterizes faith. Like King Lear, a man who lived by the natural light of reason only to have his eyes plucked out, we hear them cry,

> O, let me not be mad, not mad, sweet heaven!
> Keep me in temper, I would not be mad! (I,v)

It is well known that those who walk the high wire

cannot take a step when the lights go out, and the few who tread the heights blindfolded truly defy death. The eyes balance, situate and control. The eyes make us as the gods, and a philosophy that is erected on the rational and the necessary strives for the God's-eye view, subsuming all things under the sovereignty of the System. If you would submit all things to yourself, said Seneca, submit yourself to reason.[12] From the time of Aristotle the function of reason has been to calm the emotions and bridle the passions; we must not laugh too hard or weep too much because tears can blind us. Thus Spinoza tells us to understand, rather than laugh, weep or curse,[13] and to understand is to see.

Speculative philosophy, then, must either eliminate faith or explain it in such a way that it cannot be regarded as a passion. The Fathers of the Church who were mesmerized by Aristotle thus described faith in terms of obedience and assent, as something which could be weighed and measured by the eyes of the Inquisitor. To be sure, here lies the secret of Dostoevsky's Grand Inquisitor, the judge who usurped God for the sake of man: in truth, he wants to get rid of faith; in truth, he works not in the name of the Nameless One but in the name of the serpent.

Through the voice of Hegel philosophy finally asserted what it had dreaded to assert: the serpent was not the deceiver.[14] This, indeed, is the question that decides the relation between faith and philosophy: who was the deceiver, God or the serpent? Because the serpent makes its home in the Tree of Knowledge of Good and Evil, something should here be said about the connection between rationality and morality. The knowledge of good and evil rests on imperatives that are just as categorical as those of reason. Like reason, morality functions according to the if-then of the law of contradiction—if patricide is always immoral, then it can never be moral and therefore can never be condoned. Like reason, morality judges and controls, seeking to bring all the kingdoms of the earth under its authority —what is moral here must be moral there and everywhere. Instead of That Thou Art morality says Thou Shalt Not; instead of Yes, No.

Again, speculative philosophy walks by sight, and a sense of morality requires a sense of sight. When morality looks upon a human being and pronounces judgement, the person is reduced to an It, an object whose outward aspects are plugged into a legalistic formula in order to arrive at a verdict. Thus emerges the law written in stone. The voice that responds to the call by saying Here I Am and That Thou Art is drained into written prose, for written prose begins with the law. When the spoken word is lost to the written word, we demand an idol that is as mute as we are, a code of direction that we can see carved into a stone that we can touch. Philosophy grounded in rationality, morality and necessity is grounded in the way of the stone. It constructs geometric systems erected like the Tower of Babel stone by tablet of stone. According to legend, Galileo, the inventor of the telescope, always carried a rock in his pocket, a "reality stone," which he would cling to whenever he felt the ground beginning to crumble.

Derrida has said that the history of philosophy is the history of prose.[15] And in the Republic Plato stated that "there is from of old a quarrel between poetry and philosophy."[16] Speculative philosophy cannot but hold in contempt the spoken word, the songs of the poets and the outcries of the prophets. If faith comes by hearing, it is utterly alien to speculation. Because philosophy shaped by speculation is concerned with the universal authority of its imperatives, it cannot be bothered with the passionate outbursts of the moment. Its manifestos will have nothing to do with the internal life of the exception, with the passion peculiar to an Abraham or a Job. If the word "faith" should arise here, philosophy will pull out a measure gauged according to the dictates of recorded doctrine and look to see whether the individual in question has made the proper head-nodding gesture. In a word, philosophy has no idea of what to do with Moriah because it cannot sing or cry out, it cannot laugh or weep.

The spoken word lives between I and Thou, while the written word emerges between It and It; it belongs to the crowd, to the They. Because speculative philosophy focuses its attention on everyone and not on the Single One, it does its work by transforming the Thou into an It, the living subject into an object, a featherless biped. If God breathes life into the human being by virtue of the spoken word, reason and morality return the human being to lifeless dust through the doctrines generated by the written word. As soon as a man becomes an object, he is turned over to a market of exchange, his value determined on the basis of a system

8

of weights and measures. From Plato to Spinoza, from Descartes to Russell, there has been a kinship between mathematics and speculative thought. For speculative thought knows no truth greater than twice two is four.

Both philosophy and religion insist on having their converts; if one should fail to convert the human being into an It, the other will usually succeed. This is in fact the whole meaning of conversion. Virginia Woolf puts it rather nicely in this passage from Mrs. Dalloway:

> Proportion has a sister less smiling, more formidable. . . . Conversion is her name and she feasts on the will of the weakly, loving to impress, to impose, adoring her own features stamped on the face of the populace. At Hyde Park Corner on a tub she stands preaching; shrouds herself in white and walks penitentially disguised as brotherly love through factories and parliments; offers help, but denies power; smites out of the way roughly the dissentient, or dissatisfied; bestows her blessing on those who, looking upward, catch submissively from her eyes the light of their own.[17]

It is no accident that so many of the Church Fathers were fond of Aristotle. The proportion of reason goes with the conversion of religion, and there is no speculative philosophy that does not breed a philosophy of religion, no system that does not foster doctrine. Whether it ends up as Catholicism or Marxism, each seeks its own following. And faith is anathema to both.

Like speculative philosophy, religion seeks protection from the fire and the whirlwind, from the abyss and collisions of faith; it strives to displace cataclysm with catechism. Like philosophy, religion cannot function without its priesthood and the authority of the written word. Thus we have two sides of the same coin stamped in polished gold: the scribes versed in Greek and the Pharisees schooled in law. Both are educated in the ways of judgement. As we have seen, there is no speculative philosophy without a system of morality, and the goal of morality is to win submission by condemnation. Faith says Yes because it is steeped in

9

love; philosophy and religion say No because they are rooted in judgement. For one life is a gift, for the other a sentence.

Presence arises in the spoken encounter between I and Thou, in the voiced relation between I Am That I Am and That Thou Art. "Presence arises," says Buber, "only as the Thou becomes present."18 And the Thou becomes present only in the spoken beckoning of the Here I Am. But the written word struggles to lay hands on the moment at hand and thus hold presence captive. For speculative thought presence is something slipping by in a succession of moments, something that can be snared only in the nets of ordered categories. In order to capture the moments, a system of values is set up according to reason, ethics and necessity. Such is the operation by which speculative philosophy endeavors to replace the spoken word, the voice that says I Am, with the written word of Thou Shalt Not; such is the operation that replaces presence with a system of values.19 Having succumbed to the temptation of the serpent, philosophy insists on knowing when, where and what I Am before it can say I Am. This is the function of philosophy's coordinate systems. But since the system always displaces the I, the I never speaks; rather, it is spoken by the system. Hence there is never a voicing of the Thou—just a mimicry of the It.

Speculative philosophy, then, is a philosophy of absence. Here the thinker never seems to have enough time; he is forever trying to catch up, and there is always something yet to be done. He is never here but forever back there, always a sentence, a word, a breath behind. Like water—or like air—presence slips through all the traps and snares of speculation, lost, always somewhere else. Speculative thought cannot say I because the categories of the if-then speak for it. Since it cannot say I, it cannot say Thou, and here lies the thinker's absence. It is not that there are flaws in the net; no, it is the I's distance from the Thou that constitutes its absence, when it is stranded from God, left to struggle in vain to become as the gods. And the I is never more hopelessly lost than when it believes itself to be found, never farther from the truth than when it thinks it has found the truth.

This is the lesson to be learned from the primal myth of Oedipus, the man who is as lame as philosophy itself. Just when Oedipus feels his presence as king to be most pronounced, he is swallowed up in his own absence. In the words of the Chorus, he is like those

> That breathe on the void and are void
> And exist and do not exist.[20]

The tale of Oedipus is the tale of philosophy's collision with its own deception. The more he insists upon justice, the deeper he plunges into ruin; everything he does for the salvation of himself and his city draws him ever closer to the abyss. When he finds himself at the edge, he tears his eyes from their sockets, the eyes that had led him down the path of the clear and distinct. Who, indeed, can fail to call to mind the eyes opened by the fruits of philosophy, the eyes that were hypnotized by the natural light of Apollo? For when he is asked who blinded him, Oedipus replies,

> Apollo. Apollo. Dear
> Children, the god was Apollo.[21]

Augustine, Nicholas of Cusa, Pascal, Kierkegaard, Tolstoy, Dostoevsky, Nietzsche, Shestov—such thinkers are among those whose eyes were opened by speculative thought only to find themselves entombed by the stone wall of reason, morality and necessity. Pascal's Night of Fire, Kierkegaard's Great Earthquake and Shestov's Disintegration of the Bond of Ages all point to the realization that philosophy cast in rational rumination could not provide these men with the one thing needful. They collided with the discovery that the groundwork and the fortifications of speculation are mere illusion and that every description of faith offered by speculation—faith as adherence, obedience, good deeds, assent—comes to the most devastating of deceptions. If faith is to find its way into philosophy, then it must find its way into the philosopher. And when this happens, the philosopher and his philosophy undergo a change so radical that they may scarcely recognize themselves.

3

The singularity of the relation between faith and philosophy is this: as soon as the thinker shifts his attention to faith, his very life becomes an issue. I Am calls, and the thinker must find a way to respond, "Here I am." Indeed, the complaint leveled against speculative philosophy by figures such as Kierkegaard and Dostoevsky is that it eliminates the living, thinking, breathing individual. Spinoza's Ethics is a good example. Adopting the geometric system of axiom, hypothesis and proof, he makes every effort to systematize a truth, a reality, that will stand without him, just as the sum of the angles of a triangle is 180° whether the individual adds them up or not. But Dostoevsky's underground man realized that this spells the extinction of the single human being, crying, "Twice two is four is not life but the beginning of death!"[22] This is what we must be redeemed from, and our redemption lies in making one plus one equal one.

Thus the deception of the serpent comes out. The man who once turned to reason, morality and necessity in order to gain control over his life finds that he has lost his life. In the relation between faith and philosophy, then, salvation becomes an issue if there is to be any relation at all. In Tolstoy's Confession, for example, the life-and-death struggle forms the alpha and omega of his endeavor. Like others before and since, he saw that whenever he had subjected himself to a system of rationality his life had been eclipsed by the system, and he ultimately understood that without faith he had no life.[23]

In Kierkegaard, Tolstoy and Shestov we see what the thinker has at stake when he turns his philosophy toward faith. More than that, we see what happens to philosophy itself. Here thought becomes more literary, more lyrical, ridden with passion; here revelation displaces speculation. Says Shestov,

> When reason grows weak, when truth
> dies, when the light goes out—only
> then do the words of Revelation be-
> come accessible to man. And, con-
> versely, as long as we have the light,
> reason and truth, we drive Revelation
> away from ourselves.[24]

Such is the change that comes over philosophy whenever it encounters faith without trying to get rid of faith.

When faith truly becomes an issue for philosophy, the concern lies not in what I am but in that I am. While speculative thought focuses its attention on what it can see or touch, a philosophy centered on faith has to do with the invisible and the intangible. Here the one thing needful is rooted not in the outward gesture

12

but in the clamorings and collisions of the soul. As
Jaspers has pointed out, wherever existential thought
is at work, the content of thought as such is not so
important as what is happening to the individual in the
process of thinking.[25]

At this juncture what has thus far been intimated
should be said: whenever faith becomes an issue for
philosophy, philosophy becomes existential. In fact,
Shestov has declared, "Existential philosophy, which is
so closely united with faith that only in the presence
of and through faith can it do its work, finds in faith
that new dimension which sets it apart from theoretical
philosophy."[26] Existential philosophy begins where passion begins and thought leaves off. Its task is not to
resolve questions or to dismiss them as unintelligible
but to sustain the question and the passion from which
it arises. In the words of Michael from Wiesel's Town
Beyond the Wall,

> The essence of man is to be a question,
> and the essence of the question is to
> be without answer. . . . The depth, the
> meaning, the very salt of man is his
> constant desire to ask the question ever
> deeper within himself, to feel ever more
> intimately the existence of an unknow-
> able answer.[27]

The question may resound in the haunting Why of a Job
and the victims of the Holocaust or in the lama sabachthani of Jesus. We hear it in Tolstoy's "Why and what
next?" and in Ivan Karamazov's plea for the sufferings
of the children. And recall the prayer uttered by Elie
Wiesel: "I no longer ask You to resolve my questions,
only to receive them and make them part of You."[28]

While speculative thought seeks the calm and the
stasis of the formula and its ready answers, existential thought seeks the movement over the face of the
deep. On the one hand we have the image of Socrates
standing as still as stone for a full day while trying
to resolve a philosophical puzzle; then there is the
soul on fire in the frenzied dance of the Hasid. Faith
is made of movement, a constant leaping, and one must
be in motion in order to approach it. Where faith is at
the heart of the matter, where the question with an un-
knowable answer is of the essence, philosophy must
learn not how to explain but how to dance, like Diony-
sus or Zorba:

>Once, when my little Dimitraki died,
>in Chalcidice, I got up as I did a
>moment ago and I danced. The relations
>and friends who saw me dancing in front
>of the body rushed up to stop me. 'Zor-
>ba has gone mad!' they cried, 'Zorba
>has gone mad!' But if at that moment I
>had not danced, I should really have
>gone mad—from grief. Because it was my
>first son and he was three years old
>and I could not bear to lose him. You
>understand what I'm saying, boss, don't
>you—or am I talking to myself?[29]

Ivan Karamazov was stranded in the despair of speculation over the suffering of the children; Zorba broke loose by dancing. If existential philosophy begins in the despair of a Karamazov, it must somehow end in the dance of a Zorba. While the perpetuation of the daily discourse on virtue is so important to theoretical philosophy, the ultimate goal of existential philosophy is the dance—or the laughter—by which philosophy gets rid of itself. This is why faith poses such a danger to philosophy, for in order to make the leap, to dance the dance, reflection must come to a halt.

I have already cited examples suggesting that when philosophy shifts from the speculative to the existential it becomes a matter of life and death for the individual thinker. He strains every fiber of his wisdom, fires every ember of his passion, and yet the one thing needful eludes him. Soon he discovers that for all his effort, for all his eloquence, he is still like a man with a wooden leg: he cannot take a step without reflection. The matter of life and death becomes a matter of life for the man and death for his philosophy. Finally, without leaving behind so much as a note, he sets out one night with no notion of where he is going: in a sudden movement, in a leap into darkness, he sheds the texts he has created and the volumes he has consumed to meet his end in a Russian railway station.

In Section 2 of this essay I touched upon the relation between speculative philosophy and the written word. The effort on the part of existential philosophy to get rid of itself may be described as an effort to leave behind the written word, as Tolstoy did one night in 1910. Faith demands a philosophy made of voice, not of ink; that is, faith demands that philosophy be left behind—perhaps as a springboard, perhaps as a cumbersome suit of dented, rusted armor. "Thus writing itself is called into question," Wiesel tells us. "The truth will never be written. Like the Talmud, it will be transmitted from mouth to ear, from eye to eye."[30] Not from object to eye, be it noted, but from human eye to human eye, from one circle of darkness to another, when the two come face to face as I and Thou.

Faith is always a matter between I and Thou; it lives in the realm where the spirit breathes, by the breath of the spirit. Existential philosophy must ultimately die away from the written word because the word "Thou" can only be spoken, never written. Yet, as Buber has pointed out, "only silence toward the Thou, the silence of all tongues, the reticent anticipation in the unformed, undivided, unuttered word, leaves the Thou free and abides with it, where the spirit does not announce itself but is."[31] In the end the task of philosophy is to free itself from itself by learning how to be silent. A word unwritten is just that; a blank page is merely a blank. But the silence of a word unspoken, the silence of all tongues, is itself a kind of speaking. For the movement of faith is the movement of the word, of the unpronounced I Am of the Nameless One. The movement comes not when the word is uttered but when it is about to be uttered, ready to be said but still unsaid, now speaking and yet unspoken.

According to legend, Menachem Mendl, the Hasidic Master of Kotzk, once said that we truly shout only when we feel like shouting but do not shout. Faith teaches existential philosophy, a philosophy of outcry, to shout itself into silence. Heidegger writes, "Only in genuine speaking is genuine silence possible. In order to be capable of silence, Dasein must have something to say. . . . Here silence opens up to displace 'idle talk.'"[32] Such is the silence of passion. Recall, for example, the silence of Abraham on the way to Moriah or the silence of Jesus before Pilate. When God put His hand to the mouth of Jeremiah, He filled the prophet with the word by filling him with silence. And what is the silence of faith, the silence that shouts? It is the silence of prayer. A philosophy transformed by an encounter with faith is a philosophy transformed into prayer, prayer constituted by question.

4

The essays contained in this volume scratch a few

of the surfaces that shape the encounters and collisions between faith and philosophy. The first essay
looks at Kierkegaard's approach to the Binding of Isaac
within the context of the earlier views on the story of
Abraham's sacrifice, arguing that Kierkegaard's thinking marks a transformation of thought that makes his
approach to Abraham unique. The second essay examines
the movements that lead to what Shestov calls a "second
dimension of thought," a dimension that arises when the
bulwarks of rationality fall apart. Essay III takes up
a consideration of what existential thought does to the
relation between philosophy and literature, arguing
that wherever faith is an issue there is no significant
distinction between the two. In the fourth essay we see
how the life of the individual thinker is held in the
balance, as Tolstoy weighs the responses of faith to
the "question of life" against those of philosophy in
his Confession. The final essay explores the ways in
which the metaphysics of subjectivity found in existential philosophy may provide a basis for the parallels
between modern physics and Eastern mysticism.

## NOTES

1. See Elie Wiesel, Souls on Fire, tr. Marion
Wiesel (New York: Vintage Books, 1973), p. 52.
2. The Bhagavad Gita, tr. Juan Mascaró (New York:
Penguin Books, 1962), p. 112.
3. Soren Kierkegaard, Fear and Trembling, tr.
Walter Lowrie (Princeton: Princeton University Press,
1941), p. 52.
4. Martin Buber, Ich und Du in Werke, Vol. 1 (Munich: Küsel-Verlag, 1962), p. 158.
5. Ibid., p. 85.
6. See Buber, Hasidism and Modern Man, tr. Maurice
Friedman (New York: Horizon, 1958), p. 250.
7. Jean-Paul Sartre, L'Être et le néant (Paris:
Gallimard, 1943), p. 77.
8. Norman O. Brown, Love's Body (New York: Vintage
Books, 1966), p. 248.
9. Ludwig Feuerbach, The Essence of Christianity,
tr. George Eliot (New York: Harper, 1957), p. 53.
10. Lev Shestov, Afiny i Ierusalim (Paris: YMCA
Press, 1951), p. 191.
11. Edmund Husserl, Phenomenology and the Crisis
of Philosophy, tr. Quentin Lauer (New York: Harper,
1965), p. 110.
12. Quoted by Shestov, Afiny, p. 196.
13. Benedict de Spinoza, Tractatus Politicus in

*Opera*, Vol. 2, 3rd Ed. (The Hague: Martin Nijhoff, 1914), p. 4.

14. See Shestov, Kierkegaard and the Existential Philosophy, tr. Elinor Hewitt (Athens: Ohio University Press, 1969), p. 6.

15. Jacques Derrida, De la grammatologie (Paris: Les Éditions de Minuit, 1967), p. 406.

16. Plato, Republic, tr. Paul Shorey in The Collected Dialogues of Plato, ed. Edith Hamilton and Huntington Cairns (Princeton: Princeton University Press, 1963), p.832.

17. Virginia Woolf, Mrs. Dalloway (New York: Harcourt, Brace and World, 1925), p. 151.

18. Buber, Ich und Du, p. 86.

19. Cf. Derrida, De la grammatologie, p. 205.

20. Sophocles, Oedipus Rex, tr.Dudley Fitts and Robert Fitzgerald in The Oedipus Cycle (New York: Harcourt Brace Jovanovich, 1939), p. 63.

21. Ibid., p. 69.

22. F. M. Dostoevsky, Zapiski iz podpol'ya in Polnoe sobranie sochinenii, Vol. 5 (Leningrad, 1973), p. 119.

23. L. N. Tolstoy, Ispoved' in Sobranie sochinenii, Vol. 16 (Moscow, 1964), pp. 131-132.

24. Shestov, Umozrenie i otkrovenie (Paris: YMCA Press, 1964), pp. 63-64.

25. Karl Jaspers, Vernunft und Existenz (Bremen: Johs. Storm, 1949), p. 95.

26. Shestov, Kierkegaard, p. 223.

27. Wiesel, The Town Beyond the Wall, tr. Stephen Becker (New York: Avon, 1964), p. 187.

28. Wiesel, One Generation After (New York: Pocket Books, 1970), p. 241.

29. Nikos Kazantzakis, Zorba the Greek, tr. Carl Wildman (New York: Ballantine, 1964), p. 85.

30. Wiesel, Generation, pp. 15-16.

31. Buber, Ich und Du, p. 104.

32. Martin Heidegger, Sein und Zeit, 2nd Ed. (Tübingen: Max Niemeyer, 1929), p. 165.

## ESSAY I

## ABRAHAM AND KIERKEGAARD

Abraham, the father who raised the knife over his son, is the father of faith. As such he has been the subject of many philosophical and religious investigations. But wherever these investigations have been steeped in the methods and machinations of speculative thought, Abraham has eluded the thinker. The silence of the old man on the way to Moriah, the look of terror in the eyes of the child and the madness which moved the hand that clutched the knife cannot be captured in the nets of reflection. These essential aspects of the Akedah, or the Binding of Isaac (Genesis 22:1-14), are lost to speculation. However astute our thinking may be, we can never speculate on Abraham; we can only collide with him, or else flee to the comfort and the confines of our speculative systems.

In the Jerusalem Bible's version of Paul's letter to the Church at Philippi we read, "Work for your salvation in 'fear and trembling'" (Philippians 2:12). This is the source for the title of Kierkegaard's "dialectical lyric," Fear and Trembling (1843), a piece in which, for the first time, a philosopher departs from the firm ground of speculation and encounters the father of faith in the passion of fear and trembling. As I shall argue in this essay, it is an encounter born of a new understanding of Abraham and the sacrifice of Isaac, one which not only breaks with the traditional views of the Akedah but which reveals a relation between the movement of faith and a transformation of thought itself.

In order to see exactly how Kierkegaard marks a rupture with the past, I shall first discuss the historical attitudes toward the Akedah and the faith it reveals, including those of the Church Fathers, as well as other figures. Having established the traditional patterns, I shall then turn to Kierkegaard and the faith presented in Fear and Trembling.

1

It was not until Greek philosophy had found its way into the Jewish intellectual community that any real philosophical speculation on Holy Scripture began to develop, and then it was mainly by way of reconciling Scripture with Greek thought; Plato had defined a reality characterized by the rational and the ethical to which Scripture now had to be adjusted. Among the most prominent of the Hellenistic Jews is Philo Judaeus of Alexandria, a contemporary of Jesus. In his book on Philo's conception of Abraham, Samuel Sandmel explains that Philo

> . . . has allocated faith as something pertaining to the intelligible world, and he denies that confidence in perceptible things can be faith. This opposition between the perceptible and the intelligible, as applied to faith, serves to emphasize even more sharply that Philo's thinking inevitably seems to adjust itself to Hellenistic modes of expression. Since, in Philo's thought, God is allocated to the intelligible world, true faith operates only in the realm of the intelligible.[1]

As Philo sees it, faith is more an idea that occupies the mind than a passion that inflames the soul; and God here is not the "consuming fire" of Deuteronomy 4:24 but the God of the philosophers, the Prime Mover, rational, remote and immutable.

Philo's concept of faith is in keeping with the dualism of the Platonic view of the world which states that

> . . . first, there is the world of experience, about which contradictory judgements can be made; and second, there is the world disclosed to reason, about which contradictory judgements cannot be made. This latter world must represent the true reality, because whatever is must have a definite character which cannot be described in contradictory terms.[2]

If faith is real, then it is rational. And since the function of reason, according to Aristotle, is first of all to regulate the passions,[3] passion can only lead us away from faith.

Instead of deriving a concept of faith from a consideration of Abraham, Philo begins with Greek philosophy and then tries to adjust the Scripture accordingly.

20

Because he takes the light of reason and virtue to be his guide, it should not be surprising to find that for Philo the Akedah appears to be of little importance, except as "a somewhat embarrassing story which needed defense."[4] Pursuing his Hellenistic line of thought, Philo explains the story of Abraham and Isaac in terms of virtue. As Sandmel has indicated, Philo "believes that Abraham achieves the highest joy in the form of Isaac" and that

> . . . this joy is a divine gift to him, stemming from his virtue which has fathered it. True Sage that he is, Abraham is prepared, in his piety, to offer his joy to God. God, however, rewards Abraham by returning joy to him, because Abraham travels the road of virtue.[5]

The language of parricide has been conveniently eliminated; "take thy son" has been replaced with "take thy joy." Because Abraham is virtuous and virtue begets joy, there cannot even be a question of his losing that joy, since this would involve a contradiction. God rewards Abraham because within the if-then arrangement of the intelligible He can do nothing else. Moreover, Abraham offers his joy out of wisdom, "true Sage that he is," and not out of passion; here he looks more like the father of wisdom which fosters piety than the father of faith.

Thus under Philo the Akedah is not taken to be a paradigm for the movement of faith after all, but is rather explained along the lines of reward and punishment for piety and virtue or their absence. In his effort to achieve a balance of virtue and its reward and make the story of Abraham and Isaac intelligible, Philo tries to remove all contradiction by imposing the language of Greek philosophy on the Hebrew tale. He ignores Abraham's "God will provide himself a lamb." God does not provide—He rewards, and this because He can do no other.

Tertullian was among the first of the Church Fathers[6] to emphasize the Binding of Isaac as a prime example of the nature of faith. Writing during the late second and early third centuries, Tertullian views the Abraham/Isaac story not only as an illustration of the idea set forth in Luke 14:26, claiming that "no one should hold his loved ones dearer than God,"[7] but he considers the tale of sacrifice to be an instance of the vital connection between faith and patience. Abraham

> . . . proved his faith by patience,
> when he was commanded to offer in sac-
> rifice his son—I do not say for a trial,
> but rather for a typical attestation, of
> his faith. But God knew the man whom He
> had reputed for his justice. This severe
> command, which the Lord did not intend
> should be carried out, Abraham heard
> with patience and, had God so willed, he
> would have fulfilled it. Rightly, then,
> he is blessed because he was faithful;
> and rightly was he faithful because he
> was patient.8

Unlike Philo, Tertullian did not bring along the bag-
gage of Greek philosophy when he came to the Scriptures;
he did not assign faith to the realm of the intelligible—on the contrary, Tertullian is most widely known
for his "I believe because it is absurd." Yet we cannot
disregard the parallel between the virtuous man, who on
Philo's view received his son as a reward, and the just
man who was rightly blessed. Both seem to imagine a
calm Abraham making the journey to Moriah; he does not
hear the command with a gasp of horror but with patience. And we must not confuse patience with resignation. The patient man, the man reputed for his justice,
knows that God is just and faces merely a "typical at-
testation" of his faith, while the man who is resigned
to the fulfillment of the command and to the loss of
everything knows nothing, except that he faces a trial
that is beyond all considerations of justice.

In the third century Cyprian reintroduced the idea
found in Hebrews 11:17-19 that "Abraham pleased God because, in order to please God, he neither feared to
lose his son nor refused to commit parricide."9 On Cyprian's view, the substance of Abraham's faith lay in
his confidence that Isaac would be returned to him even
from the dead, while the manifestation of his faith lay
in his obedient action. Cyprian is the first of the
Church Fathers who dared to use the language of murder
in regard to the patriarch. For all that, however, he
still pictures a calm Abraham who neither fears nor
trembles at God's command; to be sure, faith here lies
in the absence of fear and trembling, in patient obedience. And, as Cyprian presents it, there is nothing absurd or ridiculous about Abraham's confidence that a

22

dead Isaac might rise again.

Throughout the fourth century the Fathers of the Church persisted in watering down the elements of blood and madness that haunt the Akedah. In a work from this period entitled On the Death of His Brother Satyrus Ambrose writes, "The father, indeed, offered his son, but God was appeased not with blood but with religious obedience."[10] And in a letter from Ambrose to Sisinnius (date unknown) we read,

> Through motives of high devotion and in
> obedience to the word of God, Abraham
> offered his son as a holocaust, and like
> a man devoid of natural feeling he drew
> his sword that no delay might dim the
> brightness of his offering. Yet, when he
> was ordered to spare his son, he gladly
> sheathed his sword, and he who with the
> intention of faith had hastened to sac-
> rifice his only-begotten son hurried
> with greater zeal for piety to put a ram
> in place of the sacrifice.[11]

In his account of the Abraham/Isaac story Ambrose over-looks the delay involved in the three-day journey to Moriah; concentrating on the obedience reflected in Abraham's swift action, it appears that for Ambrose the tale does not actually begin until the father and son have ascended the mountain. As he draws the sword he is empty of passion, "like a man devoid of natural feeling." It is not until Isaac is spared that a "greater zeal" stirs within the patriarch, yet even here we are to look at the piety rather than the zeal: it is not the zeal of piety but a zeal for piety.

The declaration of obedience as the prime ingredient of faith gained further support from Basil, a contemporary of Ambrose who asserted that "faith is a whole-hearted assent to aural doctrine with full conviction of the truth of what is publicly taught by God. This faith Abraham had."[12] The dubious nature of viewing Abraham as one who obeyed a doctrine or gave his assent to a public teaching is not so important as the loss of the individual to the doctrine. Because he is the father of faith, Abraham is now cast as the father of assent, and that which is publicly taught is here considered more essential than that which is privately suffered. The individual stands alone not before God but before the crowd.

When we are told that God set out to tempt or to
prove Abraham, it is usually understood to mean that
Abraham's faith was put to the test. In The City of God,
however, Augustine declares early in the fifth century
that Abraham's obedience was tested.[13] Nonetheless, he
is quick to add,

> What Abraham is to be praised for is
> his faith in the immediate resurrection
> of his son as soon as the sacrifice was
> over—faith in God's promise, given when
> Abraham refused to yield to his wife in
> the matter of casting out the maid-ser-
> vant and her son: 'In Isaac shall thy
> seed be called.'[14]

We also find this notion in Augustine's Retractions,
where he says,

> I do not entirely approve of something
> I said about Abraham: 'In compliance
> with this obedience, that patriarch,
> Abraham, who was not without a wife,
> was prepared to be without his only son
> and more than that, a son slain by his
> own hand.' Rather even if his son were
> slain, one ought to believe that he be-
> lieved that he would soon be returned
> to him by being raised from the dead.[15]

Thus after the emphasis on obedience and assent
found in Ambrose and Basil, we find a return to the
thinking of Cyprian, where Abraham's faith is not characterized by his obedience so much as by his belief in
the resurrection of Isaac. Nor was this approach soon
to be lost, for we read in the sixth-century Sermons
of Caesarius that Abraham so believed that he could say,
"I am offering my son and I will return to you with him.
So great is my faith that I believe that He who deigned
to give him to me of a sterile wife could raise him
from the dead."[16]

One cannot help noticing that the focus on God's
ability to restore life to the dead acquires a renewed
impetus with the death of Rome and the coming of the
Middle Ages; if God demanded that civilization thus
come to an end, He could also restore life to that civilization. At the same time, obedience must not be ig-
nored as an ingredient of faith because the Church
rests on obedience, and it was the Church that was to

survive the fall of civilization.

Although Augustine and Caesarius focus on the notion that a dead child might be returned to life, they do not pursue the rational and ethical contradictions involved here. Nor do they go very far in their consideration of what is happening inside of Abraham; willfully or not, they remain true to the Aristotelian fixation on the observable.

The survival of civilization corresponded largely with the revival of Aristotle, and in the thirteenth century, as Etienne Gilson has pointed out, the theology of Thomas Aquinas assumes the general form of Aristotelian science made up of conclusions deduced from principles.[17] Taking up the Aristotelian worship of reason, Aquinas considered faith to be obedience and assent in matters where reason failed to provide understanding, a kind of second best to reason.[18] Like Philo, Aquinas takes Greek philosophy as his point of departure and then tries to make the proper adjustments of Scripture; in his approach to the Akedah he is not so much concerned with the nature of faith as with the ethical questions raised by the story, but he makes no connection between faith and the ethical. While the apparent deviation from the ethical was a source of embarrassment for Philo, Aquinas explains that there is in fact no such deviation by saying, "The command given to Abraham to slay his innocent son was not contrary to justice, since God is the author of life and death."[19] If one should raise the obvious objection that in this case Abraham, and not God, was to be the author of death, Aquinas replies to this objection by assuring his reader that Abraham would never have "prepared to sacrifice his only begotten son . . . had he not been most certain of the Divine revelation."[20]

For Aquinas, the ethical and the rational remain supreme, and even God must submit, else He would not be God.[21] We must be careful to note in this connection that the God to whom Aquinas refers is not the God of Scripture, the God who is Word and Fire, but the God of Aristotle, the First Cause. As Gilson has indicated, all Thomistic proofs of God bring two distinct elements into play: the existence of a sensible reality that requires a cause and the finite series of causes ending with the First Cause.[22]

Aquinas, however, is not the only person from this period who was concerned with the ethical aspects of

the Akedah. Shortly after his death in 1274 we find an
idea which foreshadows Kierkegaard's concept of a teleological suspension of the ethical. In his two-volume
study of Duns Scotus C. R. S. Harris tells us that when
Duns Scotus raises the question of whether the moral
precepts of the decalogue belong strictly to the law of
nature,

> . . . he rejects the opinion of Thomas
> that they are either self-evident prin-
> ciples or necessary conclusions drawn
> from them, and also the corollary that
> God himself cannot grant a dispensation
> from them. Such a theory, Duns contends,
> is manifestly untrue, because Holy
> Scripture teaches us that God commanded
> Abraham to slay Isaac.[23]

Although Duns Scotus did not draw a connection between
faith and a suspension of ethics, he did turn to Scripture in arriving at his position, whereas Aquinas had
appealed to Aristotelian reason.

The tension between Duns Scotus and Thomas Aquinas
was characteristic of the growing tension between faith
and reason. By the sixteenth century the Scholasticism
which had resulted from the return to Aristotle was
fading, as was the recognition of the Church's ability
and authority to save the soul. Thus one of the distin-
guishing characteristics of the Reformation was a return to Paul's dictum that man is justified by faith
alone (Romans 3:28), and it was during this period that
Luther voiced his famous sola fide, by faith alone. The
Reformers did not take obedience and assent to Church
doctrine to be essential to faith; indeed, they were
self-proclaimed rebels in opposition to the Church. Nor
in their approach to the Akedah did they focus on Abraham's obedience as the definitive element of his faith,
(although they did, to be sure, praise his obedience to
God), but rather emphasized, like Paul, the patriarch's
belief in God's power to resurrect the dead Isaac. In
his Loci Communes Theologici (1521), for example, Philip Melanchthon writes,

> Do you think a father could have carried
> out such a harsh command against his son,
> and a son to whom posterity had been
> promised? Do you think that the son would
> have obeyed the father unless each had
> trusted in the divine mercy and entrusted

himself to it? Nor did faith deceive.
The son was saved, he was restored to
his father.[24]

Looking further among the Reformers, one may discover a hint of Kierkegaard's remark that, humamly
speaking, Abraham cannot make himself understood in Ulrich Zwingli's Of the Clarity and Certainty of the Word
of God (1522), where he states,

> Looking at it from a human standpoint
> Abraham must have thought: The voice is
> wrong. It is not of God. For God gave you
> this son Isaac, by your beloved wife
> Sarah, as a token of his friendship. And
> in so doing he promised that of his seed
> the Saviour of all men should be born.
> But if you slay him the promise is nul-
> lified, and the gift is contradicted.
> . . . No, the voice cannot be of God.
> It's rather of the devil. . . . But
> Abraham did not allow himself to be de-
> flected by such acute questioning and
> extremity, nor did he follow his own
> counsel. . . . His reason could not ac-
> cept the command, but faith withstood
> reason (Rom. 4), saying: The one who
> promised and gave thy son at the first
> can raise him up again from the dead.[25]

Turning to a third representative of the Reformation, we find still another precedent to Kierkegaard,
for John Calvin in his Institutes of the Christian
Religion (1559) reveals a sense of the terror which
hangs over Abraham:

> What more frightful thing can the human
> mind imagine than for a father to become
> the executioner of his own son? If Isaac
> had died of sickness, who would not have
> thought Abraham the most miserable of old
> men—given a son in jest—on whose account
> his grief of childlessness should be
> doubled? If he had been killed by some
> stranger, the calamity would have been
> much increased by the indignity. But for
> a son to be slaughtered by his own fa-
> ther's hand surpasses every sort of ca-
> lamity.[26]

27

Calvin's alteration of the traditional picture of a calm Abraham patiently and obediently fulfilling the command again brings to mind Paul's notion that one must work for salvation in fear and trembling. For the first time we find the trace of a shift from speculating on Abraham to being horrified by him. Rather than explain Abraham, the Reformers made the first attempts at participating in the inner event that characterizes his faith.

Of all the Reformers the one whose thought comes closest to Kierkegaard and to whom Kierkegaard most often refers is Martin Luther. Although Luther does not deal with a suspension of the ethical in the case of Abraham, as Duns Scotus had done, he does turn his attention to the absurdity attached to Abraham's faith. In his commentary on Genesis, for example, he says, "This trial cannot be overcome and is far too great to be understood by us. For there is a contradiction with which God contradicts himself."[27] That is, unlike the immutable First Cause, God is able to command one thing one minute and another the next. Like Melanchthon and Zwingli, Luther perceives the key to Abraham's faith in his trust "in the Divine Majesty" and in his belief that "He will restore his dead son to life."[28] More importantly for the present concern with Kierkegaard, Luther shared Calvin's sense of the fear and trembling with which Abraham must work for salvation. Here Luther says of Abraham, "Although Isaac has to be sacrificed, he nevertheless has no doubt whatever that the promise will be fulfilled, even if he does not know the manner of its fulfillment. Yet he is also alarmed and terrified."[29] Looking still more like Kierkegaard, Luther observes, "Everything appears to indicate a delay."[30] Luther sees that the three-day wait from the moment Abraham receives the command to the moment he fulfills it doubles the alarm and terror. For three days Abraham must count his son among the dead, all the while remaining at the boy's side and looking into his eyes when he asks, "Where is the lamb?" And this while clinging to the belief that God can keep the promise of the seed of Isaac.

The writings of Luther, Zwingli and Calvin form a major turning point in the approach to the Akedah and the faith which it reveals. Most of the commentary preceding the Middle Ages came as an apology to or a reconciliation with the rational world view represented by Greek thought. Once the concern was to assure the continuation of the Church, the individual was swal-

28

lowed up by the institution, and faith was largely identified with obedience and assent to doctrine. With the revival of Aristotle in the Middle Ages reason and ethics became the only things that could justify man, and faith was nothing more than a pious nodding of the head. The Church was in charge of the individual's soul, and there was nothing easier than to fall into the established order, which at the time amounted to a movement of faith. In Luther and the other Reformers, however, we see Aristotle replaced by Paul in a return to Scripture and to the individual standing alone in fear and trembling before God, not before the Church. Indeed, Luther declared that if Scripture should prove him wrong, he would gladly break off his rebellion. Thus the Binding of Isaac was now shrouded with contradiction—"there is a contradiction with which God contradicts himself"—and reason, if not ethics, was the temptation—"reason could not accept the command, but faith withstood reason."

But just as Luther's sola fide was soon lost to a new Scholasticism, so too was his insight on the story of Abraham and Isaac. The paradox and contradiction surrounding Abraham, his alarm and terror, appear to have been comfortably toned down, if not completely forgotten. When in the eighteenth century reason and virtue became the keys to the Enlightenment, the Abraham/Isaac episode came under attack, as might well be expected. During the Age of Reason Scripture fell under the scrutiny of reason, and it was difficult for rational men to swallow the notion that God could violate natural necessity by raising the dead, not to mention the ethical outrage at the command itself.

Among Abraham's most prominent defenders, however, was Voltaire, one of religion's greatest critics, who in his Mélanges appeals to Scripture itself in reply to the critics of the Akedah.[31] Yet unlike the Reformers of the sixteenth century, Voltaire considers the essence of faith as demonstrated by Abraham to be obedience to God. He too refused to attach contradiction to the tale, and the temptation which Abraham faced was not reason or ethics but simply disobedience to God. Nor was Voltaire the only one who at this time understood the Binding in such a manner: Hamann, whom Kierkegaard read thoroughly, also focused on Abraham's obedience in faith in contrast to the disobedience of Adam at the time of the creation.[32]

In 1843 Kierkegaard wrote the most extensive and

most penetrating study of Abraham yet to be produced. He too, however, falls within a tradition. Along with the new Scholasticism which followed Luther there arose a new reaction against Scholasticism. Early in the seventeenth century William Teellink, Amesius and Jacodus van Lodensteyn denied any connection between faith and intellectual activity or ability, and their contemporary, John Arndt, emphasized rebirth and a personal identification with God as the vital aspects of faith. Drawing on the work of Arndt, Philipp Jakob Spener emerged as the founder of Pietism, a movement which, F. Ernest Stoeffler explains, endeavored to "preserve the experiential element in Protestantism which was so obvious in Luther as well as in Calvin. Its theology was wholly centered on the written Word, that Word having to be inwardly appropriated through the Spirit."[33] Thus arises the language of inwardness and transformation in a personal relationship to God in faith. Pietism continued throughout the eighteenth century, and if Kierkegaard is to be associated with the movement, he appears in its culmination.

2

During the late eighteenth and early nineteenth centuries Sentimentalism and Romanticism emerged in reaction against the Age of Reason, and this was accompanied by a renewed conflict between faith and reason. Although Hamann and Jacobi had taken the part of faith, Kant and Hegel were the dominating figures of the philosophical schools of thought, and both were products of the Enlightenment in their respect for the autonomy of reason. Kant, for example, had placed a "purely rational faith" above a "divinely induced faith,"[34] and Hegel had argued that faith was an "immediacy" to be left behind by the advance of knowledge, a matter of intuition to be improved upon by understanding.[35]

Turning to Luther and Paul for his point of departure, Kierkegaard takes up the Pietistic tradition and its break with speculative thought. As Kierkegaard saw it, the speculative thinker is philosophically in error "because he does not provide the individual with categories within which the individual can both exist and understand himself as an existing individual."[36] The difference between the nature of his thought and that which preceded him is the difference between subjective and objective thinking. He describes this distinction in the <u>Concluding Unscientific Postscript</u>, where he says,

30

> While objective thought is indifferent
> to the thinking subject and his exis-
> tence, the subjective thinker is as an
> existing individual essentially inter-
> ested in his own thinking, existing as
> he does in his thought. His thinking
> has therefore a different type of re-
> flection, namely the reflection of in-
> wardness, of possession. . . . While
> objective thought translates everything
> into results, . . . subjective thought
> puts everything into process and omits
> the result; partly because as an exist-
> ing individual he is constantly in the
> process of coming to be, which holds
> true of every human being who has not
> permitted himself to be deceived into
> becoming objective, inhumanly identify-
> ing himself with speculative philosophy
> in the abstract.[37]

In Fear and Trembling we see Kierkegaard as one subjective thinker contemplating Abraham not as a figure who
can be subsumed under the principles of speculation but
as a "Single One" who eludes all speculation. The novelty of the manner of thought employed by Kierkegaard
in his treatment of Abraham may be seen in the emphasis
of the investigation itself, in the shift from the external to the internal life of Abraham, the life that
makes him the Single One.

One can see why describing faith simply as obedience or assent or as an "immediacy" beyond which knowledge may take us would be quite unacceptable to Kierkegaard, since these things by themselves tell us nothing about the inner life of a person. If it should be
objected that one obeys God because as all loving and
all powerful He is trustworthy and will fulfill His
promises, we can show easily enough that such an objection is groundless. First of all, Kierkegaard was painfully aware of the fact that it is one thing to assert
God's ability to fulfill His promise of Isaac and quite
another to cling to such a belief while raising the
knife over Isaac. The belief as such is not the mark of
faith; faith is rather the passion that sets the arm in
motion. Moreover, Kierkegaard understood that love is
essential to faith, whereas it is not essential to obedience.

Kierkegaard, like Paul and Augustine as well as

others, maintains that Abraham's belief in the resurrection of Isaac is an essential aspect of his faith, but unlike other commentators on the Akedah, he explores what holding such a belief means in terms of an individual's existence. Focusing on the inner life of the patriarch, Kierkegaard was the first to develop the concept of infinite resignation. While Kant's categorical imperative had rendered the life of the individual in terms of his ethical connection with the universal, Kierkegaard was the first to thoroughly deal with a teleological suspension of the ethical and the significance of that suspension in terms of the isolation of the individual before God. True, the ethical question had been considered by Aquinas and Duns Scotus, but only in connection with the problem of whether ethics always reigns supreme, and not in regard to Abraham as an individual left to the silence of absolute inwardness, completely cut off from those moral dictums which apply everywhere all the time. Finally, unlike anyone who wrote on the Binding before him, Kierkegaard takes love to be a necessary catalyst in the movement of faith as revealed in the Abraham/Isaac story. Prior to Kierkegaard love had been associated with the Binding only whenever the tale was used as an illustration of loving God more than one's family, even more than one's only son. Because his love for Regina led him to "sacrifice" her, Kierkegaard correctly understood that Abraham's love for Isaac was not subordinate to his love for God but was rather the measure of that love. Let us now consider these perspectives in Kierkegaard's treatment of Abraham and how they lead to a new way of thinking about faith.

Fear and Trembling is not a theological or philosophical treatise but, as the subtitle indicates, it is a "dialectical lyric." In the initial pages of the work Kierkegaard explains that his interest in Abraham is not that of one engaged in speculative thought but of one who seeks to grasp the shudder or the terror of thought.[38] His attention is concentrated first of all on the dread which overshadows the contradiction in Abraham's situation, and unless we take a share in that dread, as Kierkegaard did, the patriarch is lost to us. In regard to Abraham's dread Kierkegaard writes,

> The ethical expression for what Abraham did is, that he would murder Isaac; the religious expression is, that he would sacrifice Isaac; but precisely in this contradiction consists the dread which

can well make a man sleepless, and yet
Abraham is not what he is without this
dread (F, 41).

Abraham's trial of faith would neither be a trial
nor would it be one of faith without dread. Dread is
here generated by groundlessness, by Abraham's inability to justify himself in the light of the paradox. God
is demanding everything of him, everything and for nothing. The man who stood the ground of justice in his
plea for the lives of Lot's family now has that ground
pulled out from under him. And in losing all justifica-
tion Abraham is forced into silence—not the silence of
emptiness but the silence of passion generated by his
love for Isaac. Dread, then, is rather like the photo
negative of faith, the point of departure for the passion, and like faith, dread is intrinsically attached
to possibility. In dread Abraham faces the impossibility of escaping the murder without failing to make the
sacrifice, while in faith he clings to the possibility
that he might make the sacrifice without comitting the
murder. In dread Abraham faces the certainty of losing
Isaac if he should fulfill the sacrifice, while in
faith he clings to the absurd belief that he might regain Isaac only if he should fulfill the sacrifice. And
regaining Isaac here means more than putting a ram in
his place; it means descending from Moriah

> . . . to live joyfully and happily every
> instant by virtue of the absurd, every
> instant to see the sword hanging over
> the head of the beloved, and yet not to
> find repose in the pain of resignation,
> but joy by virtue of the absurd (F, 61).

Such is the rupture induced in Abraham by the encounter
with the death of his son; reality and illusion have
exchanged places. The man who had been reputed for his
justice now sees the ground crumble from under himself.
The absurd has become his sole link to possibility.

So it is, says Kierkegaard, that

> . . . when I have to think of Abraham, I
> am as though annihilated. I catch sight
> every moment of that enormous paradox
> which is the substance of Abraham's life,
> every moment I am repelled, and my
> thought in spite of all its passion can-
> not get a hairs-breadth further. I strain

33

every muscle to get a view of it—that
very instant I am paralyzed (F, 44).

In spite of all its passion—here lies the definitive
key to Kierkegaard's existential attitude toward Abraham, as opposed to the distant calm of the speculative
approach which characterizes most of the earlier methods of dealing with the Binding. Kierkegaard engages in
a passionate appropriation of the passion of Abraham,
and this is why he feels that it is not the passing of
the centuries but rather the dread and the passion in
which the deed is carried out that spans the distance
between him and the father of faith (F, 45). In order
to take a step toward closing that gap, Kierkegaard
must begin with the dread that makes Abraham Abraham,
which in turn may lead him to the dread that makes
Kierkegaard Kierkegaard. This is why he emphasizes more
than anyone before him the three-day journey to Moriah,
where every step bears the weight of the dread, the
weight of the individual's existence, and provides the
opportunity for Abraham to come to his senses, turn
away from the murderous deed and return to the world
where he had been reputed for his justice. But Abraham
did not turn back. For three days he stranded himself
over the abyss. And what, we must ask, might those
three nights have been? For if we do not ask this question, if our reading of Genesis is too casual, then,
again, we have lost Abraham between the lines.

It is by setting out with Abraham in this way that
Kierkegaard acquires a sense of the dread that makes
Abraham Abraham, and it is dread that leads Abraham
into infinite resignation, as Kierkegaard describes it.
At this point a distinction between resignation and infinite resignation needs to be explained. Job's "ashes
to ashes" is the voice of resignation. When she set out
to bury her brother and honor the will of the gods, Antigone was resigned to the death that would come of it.
We can understand Job and Antigone to the extent that
they do not find themselves in the middle of a collision between the religious and the ethical. Theirs is a
resignation marked by an equilibrium, a balance, in
that they wrong no one; they still enjoy at least this
contact with the world of their fellow men. Kierkegaard,
however, takes Abraham's resignation to be infinite because Abraham cannot be understood; he is confronted
with the unthinkable. That is, Abraham must move beyond
the horizon outlined by thought and into the limitless
realm of the absurd. His resignation is infinite because in making such a personal movement he becomes in-

finitely removed from the community. Everything that had given him the strength to live in the world has been left on shore. Thus he infinitely resigns himself to the loss of the one for whom his love is infinite, whom he shall lose by his own hand.

Both the movement of infinite resignation and the movement of faith are effected by passion, and both therefore take up where thought leaves off. Speculative thought had once defined the boundary line between the possible and the impossible, but boundless passion has now erased that line to open up the possibility of all things. Here lies the path to the God relationship, and in the light of God's command to Abraham it is the one path that can lead the lost Abraham back to the world so that the world is gained anew. This is why Kierkegaard declares, "For the movements of faith must constantly be made by virtue of the absurd, yet in such a way, be it observed, that one does not lose the finite but gains it every inch" (F, 48). Unlike anyone before him, Kierkegaard understood that the import of Abraham's trial is rooted not only in the dreadful ascent to the altar but in the return to life, to Sarah. And every time Abraham would later look into Isaac's eyes the trial would resurface.

Abraham is resigned to the loss of Isaac, yet it is not simply the loss of Isaac that is in question but the sacrifice of him. Because it is a sacrifice, a holy act pleasing to God, Abraham must make a double movement, to use Kierkegaard's phrase, so that along with the movement of infinite resignation Abraham makes the movement of faith by which he breaks through to the absurd, to the groundlessness over which his belief in the resurrection of Isaac is hanging. The absurd here characterizes the realm of infinite possibility, where the camel may pass through the eye of a needle. It must be noted that Abraham's relation to the sacrifice and resurrection of Isaac, his relation to God, is deemed absurd only from the point of view of the rationality and natural necessity which he has transcended through the infinite movement. Abraham's belief in God's ability to fulfill his promise of Isaac is absurd for thought but not for the passion that takes up where thought leaves off. Furthermore, when, in infinite resignation, the attention is directed toward the loss, it is concentrated on the finite self, on Sarah's husband who is known for his fairness and who shall see his son no more. However, in the passion which attends the resignation the individual encounters that eternal aspect

35

of himself which focuses his consciousness on the God
relationship and the sacrifice to God. The Kierkegaardian distinction between the eternal self and the finite
or temporal self may be described as a distinction between the individual's religious or spiritual life and
his day-to-day, secular life. Wherever there is a coming before God, there the eternal self comes to bear;
there the individual's life in the world, the life of
Abraham as the father of Isaac, intersects with his
life in relation to God, the life of Abraham as the
father of faith. This is the intersection, the confron-
tation, that leads him to the absurd belief that for
God all things are possible, even the resurrection of
his dead son.

Possibility, then, is rendered in terms of the
eternal, and not in terms of the finite or temporal; to
use Kierkegaard's words,

> . . . spiritually speaking, everything
> is possible, but in the world of the
> finite there is much which is not pos-
> sible. This impossible, however, the
> knight makes possible by expressing it
> spiritually, but he expresses it spir-
> itually by waiving his claim to it (F,
> 54).

There is a connection between possibility and expression, but here silence becomes the expression of the
spirit. As Erich Auerbach has pointed out, in the story
of Abraham and Isaac speech does not serve to external-
ize thought but to hide it.[39] In Kierkegaard's own effort to give voice to the significance of Abraham we
see that the word merely frames the silence of the
eternal which now accentuates the finite. Yet the eternal is not isolated from the individual's daily life;
on the contrary, "it penetrates the entire network of
his finite relations, thereby bringing them to their
full potential and meaning for him as an existing individual."[40]

Here lies the paradoxical relation between faith
and resignation. It should be pointed out, however, that
if the two are tied together in a double movement,
Kierkegaard is careful to maintain a distinction:

> The infinite resignation is the last
> stage prior to faith, so that one who
> has not made this movement has not faith;

36

for only in the infinite resignation do
I become clear to myself with respect to
my eternal validity, and only then can
there be any question of grasping existence by virtue of faith (F, 57).

By "eternal validity" Kierkegaard refers to an awareness of the trial which faces the "eternal self" before
God. It is not by virtue of faith that Abraham finds
himself put to the test, but faith is required if Abraham is to see it through and descend from Moriah to return to Sarah. In other words, faith is needed to undo
the infinite resignation and the absolute isolation
born of that resignation. Abraham, then, must undertake
not only the task of raising the knife but the task of
returning to a secular life in which the knife forever
hangs over what he holds most dear, a life shaped by
sacrifice. Thus for Abraham faith is required if he is
to make the sacrifice. And it must be a sacrifice, an
act of faith, and not simply a loss, if he is to regain
Isaac over and above his clarity of self before God.

    In infinite resignation Abraham removes himself
from himself, from the universal, and therefore from
the ethical. That is to say, he is no longer the person
who assumes a role in the community according to the
general standards that make up a community. Because his
resignation is infinite, complete and unconditional,
Abraham is recast in the mold of absolute isolation. In
this way he becomes the single individual, the Single
One, as he must, for it is only in connection with the
individual that there can ever be a question of making
a movement of faith and entering into a relationship to
the absolute God. This is what Kierkegaard calls "the
absolute relationship to the absolute." The relationship is absolute in that it is generated without at-
tachment or causal connection with anything else. Moreover, the relationship is absolute because it pertains
to God—and to Isaac—as the absolute Thou, residing
beyond all the relativistic considerations that make
the world a world. God encompasses all horizons, as
does the individual who can establish an absolute relationship to God. This is why Kierkegaard states,

        Faith is precisely this paradox, that the
        individual as the particular is higher
        than the universal, is justified over
        against it, is not subordinate but supe-
        rior—yet in such a way, be it observed,
        that it is the particular individual who,

> after he has been subordinated as the
> particular to the universal, now through
> the universal becomes the individual who
> as the particular is superior to the
> universal, for the fact that the indi-
> vidual as the particular stands in an
> absolute relation to the absolute (F, 66).

The emotional turmoil of the individual takes precedence over the reason, ethics and natural necessity
that apply everywhere all the time, because it is the
passion that brings the individual into a solitary,
personal, absolute relationship to the absolute. Individual time, or life time, displaces the chronology of
the universal chain of cause and effect; eternity displaces futurity in such a way that the relationship is
the first and the last, the one and only. And since the
condition of the eternal self is determined absolutely,
the individual is isolated in a Last Judgement, where
his spiritual _telos_ is thrown into the balances.

Thus considered, the isolation may be said to be
teleological, and it is never more absolute than when
Abraham raises the knife over his son, suspending tele-
ologically all that belongs to the universal. Indeed,
all the support which the universal might offer, all
the handrails of his existence, must be yanked away
from him if Abraham is to stand in an absolute relation
to the absolute. Furthermore, since the suspension of
the ethical occurs outside the universal, we cannot employ the categories of rational speculation in our "understanding" of it; it is not to be taken as a transgression of ethics, for example, but rather must be understood in the context of the God relationship. Because the sacrifice is religious rather than ethical,
it cannot be grounded in the ethical, and there is no
ethical imperative or direction to be derived from the
sacrifice.

It is the absolute relationship, and not a moral
transgression, which isolates the individual in contradiction to the universal and the systems upon which it
is erected. In contradiction because the universal does
not acknowledge any such isolation or selfhood, yet the
individual is so isolated only by virtue of having been
part of the universal order. In this regard Louis H.
Mackey makes the following helpful observation:

> It is only _through_ his constancy in the
> universal that he comes to this point at

which he is strong enough to be weak
before God, wise enough to be foolish
before God. He is justified by God (the
absolute) as himself (the particular),
over against himself (the universal).
Through the universal Abraham becomes
the individual justified by God over
against the universal.[41]

We may note further that since Abraham becomes the individual in contradiction to all systems of universality, there is nothing which precedes the individuality
from which it might arise: Abraham becomes the individual suddenly, by a leap. Once again we see the shift
from objective time to subjective time, from the temporal flow of cause and effect to the experiential instant of the eternal consciousness, the moment when the
individual's spiritual life is most accentuated by the
prospect of being forever lost. In the universal realm
of world and community there is no room for the sudden,
just as there is no room for the spirit; one thing always rests upon and proceeds from another, indifferent
to the passion that brings the spirit to bear.

In Abraham's case the ethical is itself the temptation, because the ethical is an expression of the
universal and as such precludes all isolated or absolute relationships. Likewise, the rational appears in
the form of temptation, since it also is an expression
of the universal, declaring quite sensibly that the
dead must remain forever dead and that all passion is
vain, if not harmful. This is why Abraham cannot speak,
why he cannot state his case, for language is public,
and as soon as he makes use of it he must speak as the
world speaks and see as it demands; as soon as he
voices the absolute relationship, it is lost to the
relative. In the world Abraham is and remains a murderer. Thus the God relationship can exist only in the silence of the passion that is faith. And if this relationship should be rendered in terms of the universal
so that it might be understood, then it has for that
very reason been  misunderstood.

Since the relationship to God lies within, and
since this is what makes the individual "superior" to
the universal, we may see why Kierkegaard says, "The
paradox of faith is this, that there is an inwardness
which is incommensurable for the outward, and inwardness, be it observed, which is not identical with the
first but is a new inwardness" (F, 79). Life conceived

externally is life situated within a system of reference points, and the expression of inwardness as an external means identifying oneself in terms of those reference points. Such a coordinate system may be found
on any personal data sheet. The notion that "there is
an inwardness which is incommensurable for the outward"
suggests that there is a something within the individual that exists apart from any outside orientation. And
this something is what makes the individual an individual; this is what comes into play whenever we take our
prayers to our closet. The inwardness of faith cannot
be given outward expression because once the God relationship is externalized, it is turned over to the
crowd. This is the novelty of the new inwardness, that
it removes the individual from all considerations of
the universal and therefore from all externalization.
In this respect it is an absolute inwardness, one that
is self-imposed in decisiveness. What is more, in the
movement of faith there emerges with the new inwardness
a new individual, one who now "determines his relation
to the universal by his relation to the absolute, not
his relation to the absolute by his relation to the
universal" (F, 80). The absolute, rather than the voice
of the crowd, is now the measure of the self. Here the
self is measured qualitatively, according to its spiritual condition, instead of quantitatively, according
to the statistical curve.

This brings us to the most important point in our
understanding of what is so unique in Kierkegaard's approach to the father of faith. When the absolute duty
to God emerges to determine the ethical duty, love for
one's fellow man or for one's only son is measured
qualitatively, according to one's love for God. Unlike
those commentators who viewed Abraham's love in quantitative terms, that is, who saw Abraham loving God more
than Isaac—and they all appear to take this stance either implicitly or explicitly—Kierkegaard tells us,

> When God requires Isaac Abraham must love
> him if possible even more dearly, and only
> on this condition can he sacrifice him;
> for in fact it is this love for Isaac
> which, by its paradoxical opposition to
> his love for God, makes his act a sacri-
> fice. But the distress and dread in this
> paradox is that, humanly speaking, he is
> entirely unable to make himself intelli-
> gible. Only at the moment when his act
> is in absolute contradiction to his feel-

ing is his act a sacrifice, but the reality
of his act is the factor by which he belongs to the universal, and in that respect he is and remains a murderer (F, 84).

Kierkegaard opens our eyes to the fact that Abraham's
love for God and his love for Isaac are in paradoxical
opposition because his love for God is the measure of
his love for his son. And since his love for his child
is what makes the sacrifice a sacrifice, it is by virtue of that love that Isaac is returned to him. Love is
the bond between the eternal and the temporal, where
the eternal Thou cuts into the Thou who stand before us.
If it requires a great love of God to perform the sacrifice, so too is a great love of Isaac required, and
not a subordinate love. If Abraham's love for Isaac is
a subordinate love; if the Thou by which he addresses
Isaac does not harbor the Thou by which he addresses
God, then Abraham is lost to the herd.

   Thus the unique character in Kierkegaard's approach to the Akedah is rooted primarily in his views
on Abraham's dread, resignation, isolation and love.
These are the aspects of Abraham from which Kierkegaard
derives the concepts of the absolute relation to the
absolute, the teleological suspension of the ethical
and the passion of faith. In this way he has avoided
the contamination of Aristotle and has revealed the
error of those who had understood faith as obedience
or assent or an immediacy beyond which knowledge may
take us. Regarding the Reformers, the Pietists and
others who had understood faith as an inward passion
resting on the absurd, Kierkegaard has brought out the
ramifications of such a view. He struggles to assume
the passion of Abraham, and in so doing he is as it
were annihilated. This is what it means to work for
salvation in fear and trembling.

3

   Having examined Kierkegaard's philosophical effort
to deal with faith as revealed in the Akedah, let us
now consider the implications which such a philosophy
may have for faith. The following insight from Cornelio
Fabro may help to make a start:

      The difficulty inherent in the act of
      faith is of an order completely differ-
      ent from that inherent in a judgement
      on some doctrine which is to be either

followed or rejected. In the case of a
doctrine, man finds a structure already
present in the object, and in his understanding he has a power, proportionate
to his intellectual level, to penetrate
and explain this doctrine. The act of
faith, on the other hand, implies a total
break with the rationality of the immediate and requires a passage into a
sphere which is absolutely incommensurable with that of the natural man even
though he be the most gifted genius.[42]

Faith is not to be understood as obedience, assent or
something to fall back on when reason fails. It is not
a belief in God or any other absurd belief per se; rather, it is a passion, as Kierkegaard describes it,
that passion which arises as the essence of the God relationship. And what is passion? It is the leap into
the abyss, the explosion into a mountain of fire, which
the Baal Shem revealed to his son Rebbe Hersh in a
dream, when his son asked him how to find the path that
leads to God. To be sure, this is the only question
that concerns the single individual, for every other
dimension of his existence is determined by the presence or absence of this passion.

    With the example of the Baal Shem's revelation to
his son we may better see how Kierkegaard's distinction
between subjective and objective thinking can affect
what philosophy might say about faith. Kierkegaard
views faith as a manner of existing, not as an object
of comprehension; there is no going beyond faith with
the advent of knowledge. Faith itself is beyond—beyond
the everyday, beyond the crowd, beyond the ticking of
the clock; but without it the day itself is lost to us,
every person is a stranger, and the ticking of the
clock is a burden impossible to bear. In short, without
faith there is no self. Thus under Kierkegaard's so-
called subjective mode of thought the life of the self
is tied to the paradox of faith, for here a man's love
for his child is the vessel of his love for God.

    Abraham is the creator of himself to the extent
that he alone creates his God relationship. This is
what constitutes the dreadfulness of the situation:
Abraham must rise ex nihilo, with no support, no substance, other than that which his passion can generate.
Faith, then, is a passion whereby the self is engaged
in a process of creating itself. Again we see a con-

trast between Kierkegaard's dialectical lyricism and the determinism—be it social, political, ideological, economical or what have you—born of speculative thought. When the self is gauged according to its faith it is reduced to nothing in its relation to God, and the man's ability to be reduced to nothing before the absolute makes him superior to the universals of the world; everything is demanded of him, says Kierkegaard, everything and for nothing.[43] The spirit appropriates through renunciation, and Abraham thus resigns himself to nothingness, to the loss of everything forever, which is what makes his resignation infinite as well as passionate.

Viewed as the paradigm for faith, Abraham is the model for defining the individual, or the self, which is the category of inwardness, since both the movement of infinite resignation and the movement of faith occur in inwardness. The individual becomes a "category" of one by becoming separate, isolated. In order to completely isolate himself within, all the things from which he normally derives the strength to live in the everyday world, all the things which provide him with certainty and direction—reason, ethics, propriety, necessity—all must be cast away, abandoned, left on shore; the eye must be plucked out. Taking an example from Kierkegaard's Training in Christianity (1850),

> . . . at the absolute the understanding
> stands still. The contradiction which
> arrests it is that man is required to
> make the greatest possible sacrifice, to
> dedicate his whole life as a sacrifice—
> and wherefore? There is indeed no wherefore.
> 'Then it is madness,' says the understand-
> ing. There is no wherefore because there
> is an infinite wherefore. . . . If now
> there is to be a victorious advance, faith
> must be present, for faith is a new life.[44]

Abraham's understanding tells him that what he is about to do is the most terrible madness, that he must return to Sarah with the boy unharmed; the temptation of the rational and the ethical would draw him out of his inwardness and turn him away from his relationship to God. Thus the Akedah can only be enacted within, and there is nothing in its outward parts which in itself might give Abraham away as a knight of faith rather than a mad killer.

43

Unlike other trials, the importance of Abraham's trial is not so much the outcome as the sustaining of the trial itself, since the trial is a trial of becoming. In establishing the absolute relationship between itself and God, the self confronts itself as a task, as something which must be created, something for which the individual is responsible. The existence which the self creates for itself is subjective existence, or existence as subjectivity; it determines, and is not determined by, necessity, and in this sense subjective existence is existence as possibility. When the self becomes itself in the God relationship, the "new inwardness" that emerges is new in that the individual is now engaged in a process of internalizing the external, rather than externalizing the internal. This means that instead of speaking as the world speaks, instead of expressing himself in order to make himself understood, the individual gives his subjective existence a spiritual expression: I believe because it is absurd. In this way the possibility of believing something because it is unbelievable finds its way into the life of the individual. Existence as possibility, then, comes about in the subjective appropriation of the objective, thus bringing the temporal into a synthesis with the eternal. "In time," says Kierkegaard, "the eternal is the possible."[45]

Because faith brings about a process of inward becoming, it raises the question of how we are to think about time. A distinction must be made between objective time and subjective time, between external spatialized time and internal life time. Under objective time, for example, the future is anticipated in the present by examining the past; we advance by looking backwards, and everything has its corresponding spatial coordinates from which we plot a spatial progression in time. Thus considered, time is inseparable from the external, as is the individual, which is to say there is no individual; there can be no becoming but only a rearranging of what is. The future is therefore farthest from eternity, as Kierkegaard puts it,[46] and it is objective time that tells us there is nothing new under the sun.

For subjective time or life time, however, the next day does not exist, and it is only when time has been thus despatialized that there can be any question of a relationship between the temporal and the eternal. Instead of anticipating and plotting the future by looking backwards, the individual here turns about and proceeds in the darkness and passion of faith without knowing where he goes. In order to make the move from subjective time to objective time, the individual must decisively break off all reflection and isolate himself in the instant.

The next day becomes nothing, the instant everything. Kierkegaard refers to the instant in The Concept of Dread (1844) when he says, "The eternal is the present. For thought, the eternal is the annulled (aufgehoben) succession—time would be succession, going-by. For visual representation, eternity is a going-by, yet it never budges from the spot."[47] In his infinite resignation Abraham obtains his "eternal consciousness," so that the instant is no longer a particle of time but of eternity; that is, the instant is the point where eternity meets tangentially with time; or, in the words of Kierkegaard, the instant "is the finite reflection of eternity in time, its first effort as it were to bring time to a stop."[48] Here we see that in objective time one moment leads to and cannot be separated from the next; in subjective time, on the other hand, one instant does not follow the other, for there is only the one instant, the decisive instant. Life time, then, is precisely the instant.

Because the individual's internal and eternal life is shaped by his relation to God, it is only in terms of the instant that his eternal life or his spiritual life is called into question; immortality lies in the instant. Here the determination of the individual's eternal condition takes place. Thus immortality does not mean living forever into the future, day after day, year after year; rather, immortality means the Last Judgement, the solitary Single One directly before God. Looking at the faith revealed in Kierkegaard's treatment of Abraham, we see that Abraham does not escape the Judgement through faith but rather comes before the Judgement, the Trial, by virtue of faith.

Within the Western tradition, the way in which we approach and think about existence has been largely determined by reason, ethics and natural necessity. Reason tells us that it is ridiculous to believe anything because it is absurd; such an assertion is unintelligible. Whatever is real is rational and can be rendered in sensible language. Ethics tells us that Abraham is a murderer, that any God who would demand the life of an innocent child is more a devil than a god. And natural necessity tells us that it is sheer folly to sup-

45

pose that a dead Isaac can be the seed of generations to come. Opposite this tradition Kierkegaard presents us with a picture of faith as a rupture with such speculation. In order to pursue the father of faith all the way to Moriah, philosohpy had to leave itself behind, just as Abraham left behind his life with Sarah, his life as a man reputed for his justice in a world that made sense. Prior to Kierkegaard the relation between faith and philosophy was at best tenuous. With the advent of his new approach to Abraham philosophy took up a new direction in its concern with matters of faith.

### NOTES

1. Samuel Sandmel, Philo's Place in Judaism (New York: Ktav Publishing House, Inc., 1971), p. 139.
2. E. T. Adams, Experience, Reason and Faith: A Survey in Philosophy and Religion (New York: Harper & Brothers, 1940), p. 251.
3. Ibid., p. 273.
4. Sandmel, Philo, p. 208.
5. Ibid., pp. 174-176.
6. The Oxford Dictionary of the Christian Doctrine, ed. F. L. Cross, 2nd Ed. (London: Oxford University Press, 1974) gives the following account of how the Church Fathers viewed the story of Abraham and Isaac:

> The Fathers, e.g. St. Clement of Rome and St. Ambrose, exalted his generous obedience in leaving his homeland; and St. Augustine loved to compare it to the following of the Word practised by the Apostles. Later spiritual writers see in it a type of the religious vocation of the individual soul. His sacrifice particularly furnished the Fathers with a model of perfect submission to the will of God even in the severest trials. It came to prefigure the death of Christ, and many writers, e.g. Tertullian, Origen, St. Cyril of Alexandria, and Theodoret, draw out all the similarities, e.g. the ram that is killed signifies the humanity, and Isaac who remains alive the Divinity of the Lord. In the Canon of the Mass, and in the prose of the Feast of Corpus Christi, 'Lauda Sion,' the immolation of Isaac prefigures the Sacrifice of the Mass (p. 6).

7. Tertullian, <u>Disciplinary, Moral and Ascetical Works</u>, tr. Rudolph Arbesmann, Sister Mary Joseph Daly and Edwin A. Quain in <u>The Fathers of the Church</u>, Vol. 40 (New York: The Fathers of the Church, Inc., 1959), pp. 166-167.

8. <u>Ibid</u>., pp. 203-204.

9. Cyprian, <u>Treatises</u>, tr. and ed. Roy J. Deferrari, FC, Vol. 36 (1958), p. 208.

10. Ambrose, <u>On the Death of His Brother Satyrus</u>, tr. John L. Sullivan and Martin R. P. McGuire, FC, Vol. 22 (1953), p. 241.

11. Ambrose, <u>Letters</u>, tr. Sister Mary Melchior Beyenka, FC, Vol.26 (1954), p. 490.

12. Basil, <u>Ascetical Works</u>, tr. Sister M. Monica Wagner, FC, Vol. 9 (1950), p. 59.

13. Augustine, <u>The City of God</u>, tr. Gerald G. Walsh and Grace Monahan, FC, 14 (1952), p. 544.

14. <u>Ibid</u>., p. 545.

15. Augustine, <u>Retractions</u>, tr. Sister Mary Inez Bogan, FC, Vol. 60 (1968), p. 165.

16. Caesarius, <u>Sermons</u>, tr. Sister Mary Magdeleine Mueller, FC, Vol. 47 (1964), p. 18.

17. Etienne Gilson, <u>History of Christian Philosophy in the Middle Ages</u> (New York: Random House, 1955), p. 379.

18. See Thomas Aquinas, <u>Summa Theologica</u>, Dominican translation in <u>Historical Selections in the Philosophy of Religion</u>, ed. Ninian Smart (New York: Harper & Row, 1962), p. 62.

19. Aquinas, <u>Summa Theologica</u>, Part II (Second Part), Questions CI-CXL, tr. The Fathers of the English Dominican Province (London: Burns Oates & Washbourne Ltd., 1922), p. 34.

20. <u>Ibid</u>., Questions CLXXI-CLXXXIX, p. 14.

21. For a thorough discussion of Aquinas and Kierkegaard see Denis A. Goulet, "Kierkegaard, Aquinas, and the Dilemma of Abraham," <u>Thought</u>, 32 (1957), 165-188.

22. Gilson, <u>History</u>, p. 370.

23. C. R. S. Harris, <u>Duns Scotus</u>, Vol. 2 (Oxford: The Clarendon Press, 1927), p. 327.

24. Philip Melanchthon, <u>Loci Communes Theologici</u>, tr. Lowell J. Satre in <u>Melanchthon and Bucer</u>, ed. Wilhelm Pauck (Philadelphia: The Westminster Press, 1964), p. 101.

25. Ulrich Zwingli, <u>Of the Clarity and Certainty of the Word of God</u> in <u>Zwingli and Bullinger</u>, ed. and tr. G. W. Bromiley (Philadelphia: The Westminster Press, 1953), p. 76.

26. John Calvin, <u>Institutes of the Christian Religion</u>, tr. Ford Lewis Battles, ed. John T. McNeill

(Philadelphia: The Westminster Press, 1960), p. 438.
    27. Martin Luther, Works, Vol. 4, tr. and ed. Jaroslav Pelikan and Walter A. Hansen (St. Louis: Concordia Publishing House, 1964), p. 93.
    28. Ibid., p. 106.
    29. Ibid., p. 95.
    30. Ibid., p. 109.
    31. Voltaire, Mélanges in Oeuvres Complètes, Vol. 30 (Paris: Garnier Frères, 1880), p. 35.
    32. J. G. Hamann, Sämtliche Werke, Vol. 1 (Vienna: Verlag Herder, 1949), p. 35.
    33. Ernest J. Stoeffler, The Rise of Evangelical Pietism (Leiden: E. J. Brill, 1965), p. 10.
    34. Immanuel Kant, Die Religion innerhalb der Grenzen der blossen Vernunft in Sämtliche Werke, Vol. 4, ed. Karl Vorländer, 5th Ed. (Leipzig: Verlag von Felix Meiner, 1922), p. 159.
    35. Josiah Thompson, The Lonely Labyrinth (Carbondale: Southern Illinois University Press, 1967), p. 127.
    36. John W. Elrod, Being and Existence in Kierkegaard's Pseudonymous Works (Princeton: Princeton University Press, 1975), p. 23.
    37. Soren Kierkegaard, Concluding Unscientific Postscript, tr. David F. Swenson and Walter Lowrie (Princeton: Princeton University Press, 1941), pp. 67-68.
    38. Kierkegaard, Fear and Trembling, tr. Walter Lowrie (Princeton: Princeton University Press, 1954), p. 26. All further references to this work will be followed by the letter "F" and page number.
    39. Erich Auerbach, Mimesis (Bern: A. Francke AG. Verlag, 1946), p. 16.
    40. Elrod, Being, p. 149.
    41. Louis H. Mackey, "Kierkegaard's Lyric of Faith: A Look at Fear and Trembling," The Rice Institute Pamphlet, 47 (1960), 38.
    42. Cornelio Fabro, "Faith and Reason in Kierkegaard's Dialectic," tr. J. B. Mondin in A Kierkegaard Critique, ed. Howard A. Johnson and Niels Thulstrup (New York: Harper & Brothers, 1962), p. 162.
    43. Kierkegaard, Postscript, p. 122.
    44. Kierkegaard, Training in Christianity tr. Walter Lowrie (Princeton: Princeton University Press, 1944), p. 121.
    45. Kierkegaard, Works of Love, tr. David F. Swenson and Lillian Marvin Swenson (Princeton: Princeton University Press, 1946), p. 201.
    46. Kierkegaard, Christian Discourses, tr. Walter Lowrie (New York: Oxford University Press, 1961), p. 77.
    47. Kierkegaard, The Concept of Dread, tr. Walter

Lowrie (Princeton: Princeton University Press, 1944), p. 77.

48. _Ibid._, p. 79.

# ESSAY II

## SHESTOV'S SECOND DIMENSION OF THOUGHT

Nikolai Berdyaev once described Lev Shestov as the product of Dostoevsky, Tolstoy and Nietzsche,[1] and in the introduction to Shestov's Speculation and Revelation (Umozrenie i otkrovenie) he tells us that Shestov was a man for whom philosophy was a matter of life and death, for whom human tragedy, terror and suffering form the starting point of philosophy in such a way that "the conflict of biblical revelation and Greek philosophy became the fundamental theme of his thought."[2] Although Albert Camus believed that Shestov had only begun to "move into that desert where all certainties are turned to stone,"[3] in Le mythe de Sisyphe he describes him by saying,

> In the course of striving with admirable
> monotony Shestov struggled incessantly
> toward the same truths, seeking to demon-
> strate without respite that the most self-
> contained system, the most universal ra-
> tionalism always ends by foundering on the
> irrationality of human thought. Not a sin-
> gle piece of ironic evidence or derisive
> contradiction which may debilitate reason
> escapes him. His one point of interest is
> the exception that lies within the history
> of the heart or the spirit. Regarding the
> experiences of a Dostoevsky condemned to
> death, the frustrated spiritual adventures
> of a Nietzsche, the imprecations of a Ham-
> let or the embittered aristocracy of an
> Ibsen, he tracks down, clarifies and mag-
> nifies the human rebellion against the ir-
> remediable.[4]

V. V. Zenkovsky portrays Shestov as the high point in the drive against secularism which had been initiated by the Slavophiles,[5] explaining that Shestov's

> . . . creative contribution to Russian
> philosophic searchings lies not in the
> often devastating force of the ironical
> comments which are scattered throughout
> his works, but in the fearless disclosure
> of all the falsities of ancient, modern,
> and contemporary rationalism, as manifes-
> tations of secularism, and the disclosure

that the autonomy of reason ('transcen-
dentalism') inevitably becomes a tyranny
of reason, so that everything that does
not fall into the system of rationalism
drops from the field of vision.[6]

Although Shestov is often identified with irrationalism, his irrationalism "forms a secondary stratum
of his creativity. His religious world must be considered primary."[7] Having been part of the general religious direction taken up by Vladimir Solov'ëv, which
reacted against the "historical Christianity" that ig-
nored the mystery of life, Shestov himself glimpsed the
terrible mystery when in September of 1894 at the age
of 28 he experienced a transformation of some kind, a
"hidden catastrophe," as Zenkovsky calls it, which led
him to break with all the truths he had previously up-
held.[8] Although the details of the occurrence remain
obscure, Shestov appears to allude to it in an entry
from his "Diary of Thoughts" ("Dnevnik myslei") dated
11 May 1920:

This year it is 25 years since the 'disintegration of the bond of ages,' or more
precisely, it was 25 years last fall at
the beginning of September. I'm writing it
down so I won't forget. The most important
events in life—and no one but you knows
anything about them—are easily forgotten.[9]

Here it must be noted that Shestov had originally been
a mathematics student who in 1889 graduated from the
University of Moscow with a law degree. Given his Jewish heritage, the law meant much more to him than simply a legal code, and the "disintegration of the bond
of ages" which led him to philosophy, literature and
religion was indeed catastrophic. It was during this
period of spiritual cataclysm that Shestov began to
read Nietzsche, who was his first real teacher. In 1900
he published a comparative study of Tolstoy and Nietzsche, and three years later his book on Dostoevsky and
Nietzsche came out.

In 1921, about a year after his self-imposed exile,
La Nouvelle Revue Française published Shestov's essay
on Dostoevsky entitled "La lutte contre les évidences."
This essay is among the first to approach Dostoevsky in
the spirit of existential philosophy; included in his
collection, In Job's Balances (Na vesakh Iova, 1929),
it is the one piece that initially called widespread

attention to Shestov. As the title suggests, he is here focusing on Dostoevsky's encounter with the stone wall of reason, ethics and natural necessity, and he takes Notes from Underground (Zapiski iz podpol'ya) to be the turning point in Dostoevsky's work. The essay characterizes a further development of Shestov's earlier approach to the great Russian novelist, whom he often referred to as Kierkegaard's spiritual double, and in it he explains what it is like to "philosophize like the underground man." The underground man, for example, rejects the notion that if a proposition is necessary, then it must be accepted. Descartes was right: what is clear and distinct cannot be doubted—as long as the right of reason to judge is not questioned. But this is just the question raised by the underground man.

The Tolstoy essay which appears in In Job's Balances, however, is more than a further development of an earlier approach—it marks a complete change in Shestov's attitude toward Tolstoy. In the study of Tolstoy and Nietzsche published in 1900 Shestov had maintained that Tolstoy had reached the abyss only to shy away from it. In the essay from In Job's Balances, on the other hand, he sees the old Count as a profound thinker who painfully abandoned everything in order to place himself before the Last Judgement. The change in Shestov's attitude was largely the result of having read Tolstoy's posthumous works.

Zenkovsky asserts that Shestov "created a lasting basis for a system of religious philosophy."[10] If this is indeed the case, then it must be said that it was very much with the help of Kierkegaard that Shestov was able to establish such a basis. His discovery of Kierkegaard led him to write Kierkegaard and the Existential Philosophy (Kierkegaard i ekzistentsialnaya filosofiya), which in turn added to the development of thought that produced what is generally considered Shestov's masterpiece, Athens and Jerusalem (Afiny i Ierusalim). In this great work Shestov rejects the claim of Gilson's Gifford Lectures that the philosophy of the Middle Ages could be construed as a Christian philosophy.

Although the publication of In Job's Balances falls immediately prior to his discovery of Kierkegaard, Shestov had already established the groundwork for his existential or biblical philosophy. Like Kierkegaard, Shestov was engaged in a struggle against that philosophy which takes reason to be the sole authority in determinations of truth. In this connection Bernard Martin writes,

> The central concern of Shestov's own
> agitated and impassioned striving in
> the last decades of his life was to
> restore to men the freedom he believed
> they had forfeited in their obsession
> with rational knowledge and the God
> who had primordially granted this free-
> dom to them and who alone can give it
> back to them. This God was the living
> God of the Bible—not the God of the
> philosophers who is a principle or a
> postulate, an idea deduced by speculative
> thought from an examination of nature
> or the processes of history.[11]

Shestov viewed Spinoza, for example, as a man who took up "the dreadful task of murdering God, i.e. the God of Biblical faith—and this by none other than God Himself,"[12] the God whose existence Spinoza had demonstrated by mathematical method. Shestov saw Pascal, on the other hand, as a man who was concerned only with the salvation of the soul, and this could come only from the God of the Bible. Martin expresses the essence of Shestov's thought very well:

> How shall men find the way to truth?
> Only, according to Shestov, by becoming
> like the author of the Twenty-Second
> Psalm who cried, 'I am poured out like
> water and all my bones are out of joint.
> My heart is like wax; it is melted in
> the midst of my bowels.'[13]

In this essay I shall examine how Shestov's philosophical bones are thrown out of joint and his heart melted like wax in his effort to break through to a "second dimension of thought" ("vtoroe izmerenie myshleniya"). Perhaps more than anywhere else, this effort is exemplified in In Job's Balances. For it is here, in Job's balances, that the second dimension of thought is laid in the balance.

1

Job cried out in a dissonance of the spheres and still he cries, "Oh that my grief were thoroughly weighed, and my calamity laid in the balances together!

'or now it would be heavier than the sand of the sea:
:herefore my words are swallowed up" (Job 6:2-3). This
s the passage from which the title of In Job's Balances is taken. Like Kierkegaard, Shestov understood
:hat "Job's significance is that the border conflicts
ncident to faith are fought out in him, and that the
rodigious insurrection of the wild and bellicose pow-
:rs of passion are here set forth."[14] Here Shestov, who
t the time had not yet read Kierkegaard, repeats Kier-
:egaard's movement from Hegel to Job in an endeavor to
nderstand the nature of faith. His task is to estab-
ish his biblical philosophy in opposition to specula-
:ive philosophy. Shestov was later to maintain that
uch a move marks the beginning of existential philos-
phy, and this is what he has in mind whenever he calls
imself an existentialist. Shestov's existentialism,
is second dimension of thought, begins where thought
eaves off, where words are swallowed up; truth must be
pprehended by the passion and the wounds, and not by
n intellect that holds reason above all else.

In Speculation and Revelation Shestov explains
:hat the difference between stopping where thought
eaves off and going beyond, into a second dimension,
ay be seen in the difference between Kant and Kierke-
aard in their reaction to Job.[15] For Kant, the focus
f the Book of Job is the moral argument between Job
nd his friends. Reason knows there is no helping Job,
:hat he ought to accept and calmly bear his afflictions,
nd that the one satisfaction he can count on is ethi-
al; it is his moral stance in the face of revilement
nd catastrophe that we are to look to. Kant ignores
:he twofold return of all that Job had lost because
eason and natural necessity will not allow such a
hing.[16] Kierkegaard, on the other hand, emphasizes
his above all other aspects of the story. The key, ac-
ording to him, is the repetition that comes in faith
ather than the Greek recollection that comes in spec-
.lation.[17] If Kant is right, says Shestov, then Job,
braham and Ivan Karamazov's suffering children are
ost. Here we find the basic motif of existentialism as
hestov perceived it, namely that Job's wailing, and
ot his moral stance, reveals a new dimension of
hought. If there is a world to be seen in a grain of
and, there is another realm to behold in a tear of
amentation. But for this new eyes are required.

In the essay on Dostoevsky from In Job's Balances
hestov tells us that the Angel of Death, who has a
housand eyes, sometimes visits a man not to take him

but to leave him with a new set of eyes, to make him mad, not in the poetic sense, where the individual is beset with eros or ecstasy, but truly mad.[18] Before such an encounter with death can occur there must be a self which can meet with death in such a way that the encounter throws the self back upon itself. This means that the individual must have acquired a sense of harmony and balance about existence, that he must have constructed a coordinate system which provides the self with direction and definition. Because the system defines the individual from without, in terms of his coordinates in the universal scheme of things, it acknowledges no individual existence; until the internal life of the individual is externalized and situated within the system it is deemed either illegitimate or nonexistent. Instead of relating itself to itself, the self prior to the encounter relates to the harmony of the order, so that there is in fact no self but merely the potential for self. Here the greatest good is to discourse daily and rationally on virtue, and to will to do otherwise is worse than error—it is madness, the madness induced by the Angel of death.

Shestov claims that for Dostoevsky the encounter did not come when he faced the firing squad or during his stay in prison; Notes from the Dead House (Zapiski iz mërtvogo doma), says Shestov, is calm and in a state of equilibrium (J, 30-31). If we compare the death of the consumptive Mikhailov in that work with the passing of the consumptive Ippolit in Idiot, we find that the paralyzing terror overshadowing the latter scene is completely absent from the Mikhailov episode, in which a quiet sadness, rather than terror, characterizes the demise: "He too had a mother."[19]

The work which signals the turning point brought on by the Angel of Death is Notes from Underground, where the narrator asserts in the opening line, "I am a sick man."[20] From the first page of this work to the end of Dostoevsky's writing one senses a tremendous, even supernatural force holding him. In his book on Dostoevsky and Nietzsche Shestov writes,

> Rending a soul ridden with terror, Notes from Underground tears itself from a man suddenly convinced that all his life he has lied and pretended whenever he assured himself and others that the most sublime goal of existence is to serve the humblest man.[21]

It is not that the most sublime goal of human existence is something else but that existence has no goal, no purpose, sublime or otherwise. Even the "humblest man" is a sham, a ruse devised to provide us with the comfort and complacency of direction and to avert our attention away from the Angel of Death; the "humblest man" is simply a convenience used to direct ourselves away from ourselves. If our goal is to see to the care of the humblest man, then life is turned into a mechanical service occupation rather than a task or a trial according to which we must create ourselves out of nothing. Instead of creating a God relationship in the sacrifice of everything for nothing, we endeavor to establish a man relationship which provides us with a compensation for our sacrifice, namely the self-righteous satisfaction of serving the humblest man. Here God fades from the picture, and the terror of Dostoevsky's outcry lies in the discovery that serving the humblest man is tantamount to the assertion that as long as I have my tea the rest of the world can go to the devil.

The reign of reason and conscience thus comes to an end for Dostoevsky when he finds that hope had been supporting the doctrine and not the doctrine hope. He falls into a state of confusion, Shestov explains; he rushes ahead without knowing where he is going and awaits something without knowing what it is (J, 34). The doctrine no longer tells him which direction to take or what to expect. The Angel of Death has revealed to him his lost condition, and the state of being spiritually lost opens up the prospect of having a self in which there is something eternal, something which must be brought into a relationship with the temporal. So it is, says Shestov, that Plato failed to visit the condemned Socrates not because Plato was ill, as tradition has it, but because he could not see how Anytus, Meletus, the jailer and the hemlock could prove mightier than the truth in Socrates (J, 169). Yet it is the truth in Socrates, the truth of reason and virtue, that renders him powerless before the hemlock, just as Dostoevsky's underground man fell powerless before the stone wall.

Like Dostoevsky, Shestov collided with the realization that "twice two if four" is a principle of death. It is only after having adopted the principle, however, that one may come to see it as a principle of death; only after having consumed the forbidden Fruit does the man discover that he will surely die. It is the fallen man who encounters death, as his eyes are opened and he sees that the Tree of Knowledge is not the Tree of Life.

57

The encounter with death and the discovery of the serpent's deception, the deception of speculative thought, presupposes itself precisely at the moment it occurs; it cannot happen until it happens, and this is what gives it the abruptness which evokes the horrified "Can it be?" The hand that reaches for the Fruit is the hand that refuses to be drained of life. The Fruit is devoured, we see the life draining, and again, more desperately than ever, we refuse. For life we plead with death.

This brings us to Shestov's emphasis on the connection between freedom and the Fall. The essence of knowledge, he tells us,

> . . . is limitation; this is the meaning of the biblical legend. Knowledge is a capability, a constant preparedness to look around, ahead and behind. It is the result of the fear that if you do not look to see what is around you, you will fall prey to a dangerous and insidious enemy (J, 226).

Knowledge defines a field of vision; the eyes are opened when the Fruit is consumed. So it was that after he had fallen into a well while walking along and contemplating the heavens, Thales resolved to never again walk about at random but to always look carefully at the ground beneath his feet. Thus the birth of speculative philosophy. Moreover, when the eyes of the first man and woman were opened they were ashamed, for with the rational there is the ethical. Both judging and the ability to judge go hand in hand with being as God. But God Himself is the first to be judged by the fallen man; knowing good and evil, he sees that God's world is not good. And as soon as we judge God we lose Him, so that there is in fact no being as God but only being without God. Hence in a reversal of Hegel's claim, Shestov asserts that the serpent, and not God, was the deceiver: "The serpent said to the first man: you will become as gods, knowing good and evil. But God does not know good and evil. God does not 'know' anything; God creates everything."[22]

In losing God man loses his freedom, for both he and God become constrained by the necessary and universal truths of reason and ethics; death becomes a certainty, a natural necessity. Here we find that man's relationship to God cannot be one of dependence but can exist in freedom alone. Death is as imposing as the law of contradiction; in order to exist just once in this world, it is necessary and certain that the individual will never exist again. Says Myshkin when speaking of an execution in The Idiot,

> The primary and greatest pain is perhaps not in the wounds but in knowing for certain that in an hour, then ten minutes, then half a minute, then now, this instant, the soul will leave the body and the man will be no more; and this is certain—that's the main thing, the certainty.[23]

The force of these words is amplified even more when Myshkin later says,

> Just think, to this day it is still argued as to whether the head when it is cut off may for a second afterward know it has been cut off. What a realization! And what if it lasts five seconds![24]

Here perhaps more than anywhere else Dostoevsky brings out the dramatic distinction between the intense concentration of self within the instant of life time and the loss of self within the ticking immensity of objective time. We also find this drama enacted in Anna Dostoevskaya's Reminiscences, where she quotes Dostoevsky's own account of how he was recalled to life on the day he faced the firing squad:

> As I watched the preparations taking place, I knew I had no more than five minutes to live. But those minutes seemed years—decades—so much time, it seemed, still lay ahead of me! . . . Suddenly I heard the drum sounding retreat, and I took heart. My comrades were untied and brought back from the execution posts. A new sentence was read. I was condemned to four years at hard labor. That was the happiest day of my life.[25]

Once the Fruit becomes the forbidden Fruit, freedom becomes more than a man can bear; the fear which rises in freedom is a fear of nothingness and groundessness, a fear of chaos and unlimited possibility. The one way to gain the ground and the ability to see

whether it is still there is to do that which is forbidden, for this alone gives the individual a sense of
direction. The prohibition becomes the single point of
reference; it gives the free man a limited possibility,
which in turn gives substance and outline to the state
of innocence. Yet the substance and outline are sustained only by acting on the prohibition, which means
acting against it and surrendering freedom.

The Fall occurs in a swoon, or better, in an attempt to come out of the swoon of freedom. Shestov
writes,

> Here lies the meaning of the 'Fall of man.'
> In an apparition of emptiness, in a vacu-
> ous Nothingness he suddenly begins to see
> an omniscient necessity, according to
> which everything the fallen man does for
> his salvation only leads him to ruin.26

If it is the fallen man who encounters death, it is
equally the man who has exchanged the terrors of freedom for the reassurances of necessity; yet the encounter awakens in him a new terror, one that holds no hope
for reassurance, for it arises from the very necessity
which had promised something to stand on. The horror,
as Shestov expressed it, emerges when we discover that
"in the Bible God created a living man out of lifeless
dust, but our reason strives with all its might to return the living man to lifeless dust."27 The second dimension of thought, then, attempts to breathe life into
the dust of man.

We now come to the sudden, which, as Shestov indicates in his book on Kierkegaard, is "the implacable
foe of 'understanding.'"28 The sudden emerges as an in-
terruption in the chain of cause and effect, of the if-
then; time is thrown out of joint. The sudden is essential to the second dimension of thought because it is
what makes it an awakening from the continuum of sleep
imposed upon us by reason. The goal of knowledge directed by reason, says Shestov, is to banish from life
all that is abrupt or unexpected, since only then will
man cease asking questions and become as God (J, 157).
Thus we devise a world that rests on statistics, and by
adopting the principle of "twice two is four" we imagine that we omnisciently and omnipotently embrace the
sum of existence. We strive for predictability, for the
God's-eye view.

60

For Tolstoy, the sudden appeares one night in Arzamas, when he is overcome by a consuming fear of death, an incident which Shestov believes to be the key to all that Tolstoy wrote after his 50th year (J, 100). What is suddenly upon the individual is the madness which comes with the eyes obtained from the Angel of Death. Again turning to Tolstoy, Shestov relates three times in Tolstoy's early years when symptoms of the madness began to surface. The first attack came when the lad Tolstoy was lying in bed one night, confident that all was right with the world. Suddenly he heard a nurse and a house steward arguing, and, terrified, he buried himself under the blankets. The second onslaught came when the young Lev Nikolaevich began sobbing uncontrollably upon seeing a boy severely beaten, and on the third occasion he cried and beat his head against the wall when his aunt could not say why Christ had suffered so (J, 96-97). One may recall Ivan Vasilevich in Tolstoy's After the Ball (Posle bala), who also witnessed a beating, saying,

> I was overcome by such shame that, not knowing where to look, it was as if I were the one exposed to such horrid actions. . . . In my heart there was an almost physical torment, to the point of nausea, so that I staggered a few times, and it seemed that something was torn from me by all the terror that entered into me from the spectacle.[29]

So it was that Tolstoy came to "pose questions whenever and wherever our whole being is convinced that no such questions may be asked, for there are no answers and there never will be."[30] Why the fighting, why the beating, why Gethsemane?

Shestov writes,

> When 'chance' leads us to the edge of the precipice, and when, after many years of a carefree, peaceful life there suddenly arises before us, as in Hamlet's case, a terrible kind of 'to be or not to be,' hitherto never even imagined possible, it begins to seem that something new is directing and determining our actions. Ordinary determinism, with its striving for 'natural' explanations, does not want to take note of this, for its

                    whole task consists of not going beyond
                    what it is used to considering intelli-
                    gible (J, 193).

The limits of the intelligible are the limits of the
natural light, which is the tempter; the fallen man is
a sun worshiper, an adherent of the Apollonian and the
illusion it provides. In the Copernican universe there
is no room for a freedom lying within the darkness of
introspection. The sun is at the center, and we bask in
its light, seeking the center. But even though the eyes
appear to be opened when the Fruit is eaten, like Peter
in Gethsemane, we are in fact overcome with sleep.

     In Athens and Jerusalem Shestov compares the lie
of the vision acquired by eating the Fruit to Plato's
allegory of the cave: the things which knowledge leads
us to see have only a shadow reality.[31] The Angel of
Death alone can shake the soul from its sleep, and
this, according to Shestov, is the source of Plotinus'
insistence on the need for an awakening (J, 320). To be
sure, Shestov claims that the awakening was the whole
object of Plotinus' philosophy (J, 333). And so "when
the soul nears the authentic reality terror overwhelms
it; it feels as though it were being submerged into nothingness, as though it were perishing" (J, 307). To
approach the "authentic reality," the reality opened by
the second dimension of thought, is to depart from the
system erected on reason, ethics and natural necessity.
The individual feels as though he were sinking into nothingness because the departure from the system strips
him of the coordinates which had previously situated
him in the world. Therefore when the self is thrown
back upon itself in inwardness, it is in the first instance cast from being into nothingness. And nothingness is the realm from which the second dimension of
thought arises.

                              2

     "Ivan Il'ich saw that he was dying, and he was in
constant despair."[32] Once the Angel of Death has paid
its visit and has left us with new eyes, death is there,
continually the last, like a judge who judges without
law. The onset of despair creates a condition in despair of itself, a malady of the spirit nourished by the
impossible and by the questions that have no answers.
The questions render everything else illusory by bringing out the illusion of the Apollonian, and the illusion now serves as a background for the silhouette of

                             62

the dark reality, the black bag that yawns before us.
Seeking an expression of despair, we merely speak a-
round its emptiness, trying to give it shape with our
words.

Going a bit further with Ivan Il'ich, we read,

> Can it be that <u>it</u> is the only truth?
> . . . And what <u>was</u> worst of all was that
> <u>it</u> was turning him toward himself, not
> <u>so</u> he could do something, but merely to
> have him look at it, directly into its
> eyes; and looking at it and doing no-
> thing, he was in unspeakable agony.[33]

The onset of despair is characterized by the manner in
which death throws the self back upon itself; the self
does not observe death in the world but in itself.
Death casts the individual in the mold of outcry and
effort, but in despair the effort is forever frustrated.
The anguish arises not simply in the face of death but
in the face of one's inability to do anything. For in
order to act, in a very important sense of the word,
the action must be of some consequence, but to the man
in despair nothing can be of consequence; there is only
death, and death will come without our help. We do not
know what to do with our hands; they are a clutching
encumbrance, and as Shestov points out, it is logic itself that prevents us from doing or even knowing anything.

Logic and reason make a master of man, a judge;
having devoured the Fruit, man judges God, loses Him
and sets out to subdue the earth. It is man as master,
as the wielder of power by virtue of reason, who in
despair is rendered powerless by reason. In his unique
discussion of Tolstoy's Master and Man (Khozyain i rabotnik) Shestov explains that Nikita is equally ready
to die or to go to sleep because he has never been glo-
ified, and he calls nothing and no one to account; unlike Brekhunov, he has never been a master (J, 135).
Also unlike Brekhunov, he has never failed to place his
trust in God, the Great Master (Glavnii Khozyain), and
he is therefore confident that he is never alone. In
Nikita we have an instance of an individual whose existence is not shaped by reason, ethics or natural necessity. He has never placed truth above God—God alone
is the Great Master. He is a man of faith.

Even after Brekhunov has broken with his past in

the face of freezing to death and has set out to save
Nikita, he is still in a sense the old Brekhunov, the
one who needs to do something to avoid staring it in
the eyes. But he is never actually able to do anything
until he does something that ends all further action,
something which violates the laws of nature and rationality: he gives up his own life in order to save Nikita,
and precisely in this sacrifice he finds a surcease of
forlornness. "It seems to him that he is Nikita and Nikita is he, and that his life is not in himself but in
Nikita."[34] Thus he kicks loose the life that had held
him by the heels over the void, and in doing so he is
able to act for the first time in his life.

Insofar as action establishes a bond between the
individual and other people, the impotence to act isolates, and still another question arises: "Forlornness,
abandonment, impenetrable darkness, chaos, the impossibility of foresight, complete ignorance—can a man endure this" (J, 130)? Yet this is exactly what the man
in despair must endure. Having lost God, both Brekhunov
and Ivan Il'ich were thrown outside of a life shaped by
reason when visited by the Angel of Death. Shestov correctly observes that because they were unable to do
anything, they were left to utter solitude, cut off
from society and action, the sources from which we normally draw the strength to live (J, 122). If Dostoevsky's ridiculous man learned that "truth is attained
only in torment,"[35] the greatest torment lies in the
feeling of having been abandoned, in the lama sabachthani of a suffering God crying out from the depths of
a suffering humanity. Says Shestov,

> When there resounded the cry, 'My God,
> my God, why have you forsaken me?' it
> was as if people were supposed to stop
> and think only of how to answer this
> 'question.' People did just the oppo-
> site; they lay with all their weight
> on the One who asked such a question
> and smothered both Him and His suppli-
> cation. If it was He who asked, you see,
> then someone else must in equal measure
> resolve the question.[36]

As Shestov sees it, this is precisely the question
that impels us toward a second dimension of thought.
More than that, it is the question which brings us before the Last Judgement. So it was that Ivan Il'ich,
who despaired of the absence and cruelty of God, faced

a judgement unlike any he had known as a judge. While
Ivan Il'ich had judged others according to legality,
under the Last Judgement legality is itself the transgression. "'Legality' and 'regularity' and 'propriety'
are condemned as mortal sin," says Shestov. "They are
condemned precisely for their autonomy, for the fact
that having been created by man, they have dared the
pretense of eternal being" (J, 129). Under the Last
Judgement, then, the individual is first of all called
to reckoning for having judged according to the rational and the ethical; he is called to reckoning as a fallen man. As Shestov states it,

> Reason presents its demands without
> regard to the heart, and so does the
> heart without regard to reason. What
> is this mysterious 'heart?' With Job
> it says: if my grief were laid in the
> balances it would weigh heavier than
> the sand of the sea. Reason replies:
> the grief of the whole world cannot
> outweigh even a single grain of sand
> (J, 297).

The difficulty that remains, therefore, is to put an
end to the despair and find a possibility of tipping
the balances. Thus the struggle for possibility is an
essential aspect of the second dimension of thought.

3

In an effort to bring out the distinction between
the two dimensions of thought—that is, thought governed by necessity and thought struggling for possibility—Shestov places Spinoza's "laugh not, weep not,
curse nothing, but understand"[37] against Pascal's "seek
with lamentation."[38] Spinoza's intelligere (understand),
according to Shestov, means imagining the world as one
which functions on the basis of eternal, immutable and
rational laws, where even God is not exempt from the
laws (J, 13). Whatever is real is rational, and whatever is rational is necessary. Thus the object of
Spinoza's most famous work, the Ethics, is to trace the
path from natural knowledge, employing the methods of
mathematics, to an "intellectual love of God," a "love"
which is the child of reason. Here Shestov poses a
question:

> If we make judgements about God, the
> soul and human suffering in the same

65

way we make judgements about lines,
planes and objects, then what gives
us the right to demand or even advise
men to love God and not planes, stones
or cubes (J, 255)?

One may answer Shestov by saying we should love God instead of planes, stones or cubes because God is all
planes, stones and cubes, all life, all existence; loving God means loving everything. The difficulty, however, is that all things are not possible for planes,
stones and cubes, for the rational and necessary God.
He cannot return Isaac or the children of Job. Man and
the Son of Man have nothing to appeal to, and Job's
grief is altogether in vain; the lama sabachthani is
left to the stones. Let us therefore understand the
stones and the sand of the sea, for "the more we understand individual objects," says Spinoza, "the more we
understand God."39

On Spinoza's view all passion must be overcome,
and we must submit to the rational element in ourselves
because only then shall we be free:

The impotence of man to govern or re-
strain the emotions I call "bondage,'
for a man who is under their control
is never his own master, but is mastered
by fortune, in whose power he is, so
that he is often forced to follow the
worse, although he sees the better before him.40

And the more reason is perfected, the less we fear, the
less we tremble:

For the ignorant man is not only agi-
tated by external causes in many ways,
and never enjoys true peace of soul,
but lives also ignorant, as it were,
both of God and of things, and as soon
as he ceases to suffer ceases also to be.
On the other hand, the wise man, in so
far as he is considered as such, is
scarcely ever moved in his mind, but,
being conscious by a certain eternal
necessity of himself, of God, and of
things, never ceases to be and enjoys
true peace of soul.41

For Spinoza, it is the ignorant man, the man who does not understand, who, like Tolstoy, is consumed by a fear of death one night in Arzamas, who seeks Abraham in the dread of Abraham, or who is agonized by the sufferings of the children, as Ivan Karamazov was.

But if an individual may be determined by his emotions, he may equally be determined by reason, ethics and natural necessity and may therefore be lost to their dictates. This is why Shestov says, "Reason, or rather the wisdom born of reason, sees the essence and foundation of existence in obedience and endures absolutely no 'selfhood,' no self-sufficiency or independence" (J, 360). Reason endures no otherness. Here we also see why Shestov takes Spinoza, rather than Scripture, to be teaching obedience and piety, which Spinoza had attributed to Scripture.[42] According to Shestov, speculative philosophy never asks the question which Dostoevsky poses: is it true that reason alone determines what is possible and what is not (J, 48)? And the struggle for possibility is a struggle to answer this question in the negative.

Turning to Pascal, to seek with lamentation is to discard reason and necessity as the keepers of the keys or as the sole authorities of truth precisely because of the "peace of soul" they bring; this "peace" is the peace of the sleep induced by the Fruit, the sleep of Peter in Gethsemane. To seek with lamentation means making Job's words our own; it means internalizing the instant and thereby making contemporary the sufferings of Job and of Jesus. In the Pensées we read,

> Jesus is in a garden not of delights,
> like the first Adam who lost himself
> and the whole human race, but in one of
> agony, where he saves himself and the
> whole human race. He suffers this pain
> and desertion in the horror of the night.[43]

And He continues to suffer. Reason declares: here is the sand, but the suffering of Job has long since faded away. Lamentation replies: here is the suffering of Job despite the passing of the sand. But the power of reason is formidable, and as long as we are under its spell, life seems impossible without it. So it is that the most striking aspect of Pascal's philosophy, as Shestov viewed it, "is his attempt to free himself from the power of reason" (J, 291).

In the light of Spinoza's assertion that "it is not of the nature of reason to consider things as contingent but as necessary,"[44] we see in Pascal's struggle against reason the struggle for possibility unlimited by necessity. If there is a single definitive characteristic about the struggle, it is this: by all that is conceivable the endeavor is doomed to miscarriage from the start. Because reason always justifies itself as the ultimate judge once it appears as such, "Pascal thought only of how to debilitate our proud, self-styled reason, of how to remove from it the power to judge God and people" (J, 265). The natural light teaches us that only what is clear and distinct is true; Pascal believed that clarity and distinctness hide the truth. Paraphrasing Pascal, Shestov writes,

> If today the truth were revealed from
> under all veils and presented to man,
> he would not recognize it. For according
> to the 'criteria' for truth, or the con-
> junction of those signs which, our con-
> ventions tell us, separate truth from
> lie, he would be compelled to call it a
> lie. Moreover, he would be convinced that
> it is not only useless but harmful to
> people (J, 265).

The truth referred to here is the truth revealed in the outcries of Job, truth rooted in despair, accessible only to the second dimension of thought. And it is not only the despair that is useless and harmful but the abyss to which despair leads us.

Shestov believed that like Nietzsche, Pascal owed his philosophy to his pain, to his sleepless nights (J 271-272). The language of Pascal is in fact more that of a prophet than a philosopher; he "argues" more from revelation than from speculation or analysis. As Shestov has pointed out in Specualtion and Revelation, "To the prophet, the all-powerful God, Creator of heaven and earth, is above all things, and then comes truth. To the philosopher, truth is above all things, and the comes God."[45] Thus described, we would have to take Pascal to be a prophet. And in the realm of the prophe the realm of the abyss, lies the second dimension of thought.

The prophet lives in ignorance, in silence; he strains to hear the word of God and struggles to find the voice of possibility. Rather than pursue the spacial distance of objective thought as the philosopher does, the prophet seeks the subjective instant that draws the eternal into the temporal. The pursuit of spatial distance is a visual activity; spatial perception is visual, and the opening of the eyes is no small detail in the story of the Fall. The instant, on the other hand, is characterized by blindness, by the snuffing out of the natural light in the "finite reflection of eternity in time," and the prophet must rely on his hearing. This is why Thorleif Boman brings out the visual orientation of Greek thought opposite the aural orientation of Hebrew thought. He notes, for example, that

> . . . the Greek element in Philo's
> thinking achieves expression not least
> in the fact that where in his Bible he
> comes to an expression where God speaks
> to the ear of man, he is immediately
> very careful to eliminate God's speaking
> and to replace the hearing with a seeing
> and what is more with a seeing through
> the eyes of the soul. The change of ears
> into eyes and further into eyes of the
> soul is a motif that appears frequently
> in Philo.[46]

The struggle for possibility, then, is not a struggle to see the light but to hear the voice.

While Spinoza set out to prove "the God of the philosophers," Pascal wrote of the God of Scripture, "We know neither the existence nor the nature of God."[47] Proof finalizes and creates stability; if God can be proven, then we may breathe more easily, or so thought those who devised the various proofs of God. Reason has set up arguments for God in its quest for stability, and it is reason that assigns the predicate of existence to God. Instead of creating possibility, proof eliminates it, for the language of proof is the language of necessity, the language of certainty and direction, the language of the if-then. The individual does not struggle to establish the possibility of God's existence but, again, struggles for the possibility of creating a self within a God relationship. "To say God exists," Shestov writes, "is to lose Him" (J, 90). When God is proven by reason, He is God by the grace of reason. It is not a question of determining whether God truly exists but whether the individual has truly established a God relationship.

Shestov believed that subjecting God to reason is so attractive because otherwise there could be no assurances. But the harder we strive for the formula that reassures or for the structure that carries us to heaven like the Tower of Babel, the greater the miscarriage of communication and the confusion of tongues. Thus we read is Shestov's Potestas Clavium,

> It seems to me that it is enough to ask a person, 'Does God exist?' to immediately make it impossible for him to give any answer to this question. And I believe that all who have answered it, affirmatively or negatively, spoke of something quite other than that about which they were asked. There are truths that one can see but cannot show.[48]

Hence the truths Tolstoy attempted to reveal to others did not work for himself. "The only thing left for him is to run, run, run, without looking back, having forgotten what lay behind, and without looking to see what awaits him ahead" (J, 115).

Paradox and contradiction characterize the second dimension of thought, and these must be dwelt upon, not formulated. This is what attracts Shestov to Plotinus and leads him to the assertion that to study Plotinus is to destroy him (J, 308). Instead of looking for arguments in the Enneads, we must experience what he experiences, making his voice our own. Karl Jaspers notes, for example, that nowhere in the cosmology of Plotinus is there an empirical or logical derivation from a given premise; he emphasizes instead those moments of solitude when we face God alone.[49] For Plotinus, God is not an object of knowledge or proof or even of thought. God, or the One, says Plotinus, "is neither intellect nor intelligible. . . . For, again, since knowledge of other things comes to us from intellect, by what sort of simple intuition could one grasp this which transcends the nature of intellect?"[50] As Shestov points out, it is not that Plotinus loses trust in reason; rather, he makes it his servant (J, 366). The truth of such thinking, Jaspers correctly observes, lies not in logical operations but only in our own existence; we agree or disagree to the extent that we perceive in it our own existential potentialities.[51] Again, this is the sort of perception that requires new eyes. Potentiality means possibility, and possibility must be sought at the edge of the abyss to which reason and necessity

ring us, where we begin to probe the unknown limits,
here we plunge into the uncertainty which is the
bsurd.

Here lies the realm of faith as well as that of
ife. Reading in <u>Athens and Jerusalem</u>, we find that
ike Tolstoy, Shestov took faith to be the source of
ife:

> For the prophets and the apostles, faith
> is the source of life; for the philoso-
> phers of the Middle Ages enlightened by
> the Greeks, faith is the source of know-
> ledge as we understand it. How can one
> fail to recall the two trees planted by
> God in the Garden of Eden when the world
> was created?[52]

s we near the edge of the abyss, we near the fringes
f creation. We stand between the two trees no less
han Adam, but with a difference: the Garden is Geth-
emane, for it is here that the passion of the struggle
or possibility is enacted—we have already been cast
ut of Eden. In his book on Kierkegaard Shestov writes,

> Faith is not reliance on what has been
> told us, what we have heard, what we
> have been taught. Faith is a new dimen-
> sion of thought, unknown and foreign to
> speculative philosophy, which opens the
> way to the Creator of all things, to the
> source of all possibilities, to the One
> for Whom there are no boundaries between
> the possible and the impossible.[53]

hus the struggle for possibility has led us to the
rink of the unknown, and in so doing it has created a
ontext for the movement of thought into a second di-
ension, the movement of faith.

4

Shestov relates Abbot Boileau's account of Pas-
al's perpetual fear of turning his gaze toward his
eft because of the abyss awaiting him there. Whenever
e sat down he would move his chair a bit to the right
n order not to fall into the void. Shestov, however,
akes a slight amendment to Boileau's anecdote: he
eels certain the abyss was there but insists it was
ot on Pascal's left—it was beneath his feet (J, 272).

While Tolstoy at the end of his Confession found himself hanging over the abyss in a dream, Pascal lived in
the continual presence of it; and as the void opens, so
does a new dimension of thought, thought which is no
longer governed by the law of contradiction. Men like
Pascal and Nietzsche, says Shestov, are of another
world. They dwell above the abyss, while we inhabit the
earth. We seek the center, the path of least resistance;
they lived in daily torment (J, 273). The abyss is the
nebulous condition formed by the outcries and the questions with no answers; the task is to sustain the questions rather than eliminate them, and this is the daily
torment—we must keep the abyss beneath our feet.

Although the movement into the second dimension of
thought carries us over the abyss, it is possible only
in the presence of the questions and the torment. The
annihilation of speculation is therefore propelled by
passion. The individual kicks loose the life that had
held him by the heels and in so doing regains a new
life supported not by the groundwork of reason, ethics
and necessity but by the passion. Death is chosen for
the sake of a new life, so that the encounter with
death is now qualified by choice, by the decisiveness
of the instant. The focus of existence is thus shifted
from the result to the process; the agony is the sole
guarantee.

Loyola and Luther were irreconcilable enemies,
Shestov tells us, yet "both taught that only the person
who is lost in eternity and has been left to himself
and his fathomless despair is capable of directing his
eyes toward the ultimate Truth" (J, 219). The path to
faith has its beginning at the stone wall, where all
other paths come to an end, and only the person who is
lost can find it. Here too lies the shift from theoretical or speculative philosophy to what Shestov refers
to as biblical, existential or religious philosophy. In
the former category he places Aristotle, Spinoza, Kant
and Hegel; in the latter Kierkegaard, Dostoevsky and
Tolstoy. The difference may be expressed in various
ways. One distinction is between the Greek concept of
recollection, whereby everything has come to an end
simply to be recalled, and nothing begins, and Kierkegaard's concept of repetition, whereby everything begins and nothing is at an end. In more fundamental
terms, the distinction which Shestov makes is that
which Boman describes as the difference between Greek
and Hebrew thought. "If Israelite thinking is to be
characterized," he explains, "it is obvious first to

72

call it dynamic, vigorous, passionate, and sometimes quite explosive in kind; correspondingly Greek thinking is static, peaceful, moderate, and harmonious in kind."[54] If Boman's distinction should appear too simplistic, one may recall Erich Auerbach's comparison of Homer with the Abraham/Isaac story. In Homer, says Auerbach, language serves to reveal thought, while in the story of the sacrifice of Isaac language only conceals thought. In the Greek style everything is in the foreground, while in the Hebrew all is moved to the background.[55]

Shestov himself draws this Greek/Hebrew line of demarcation. To be sure, the title of his most famous work is <u>Athens and Jerusalem</u>, where he states that the opposition between speculative and biblical philosophy takes its most abbreviated form in Socrates' "the greatest good of man is to discourse daily on virtue" set against Paul's "whatever is not of faith is sin."[56] In Socrates we see the concept of an eternal and immutable Good which lies in the understanding of the ethical. Everything rests on the ethical, on the knowledge of good and evil, and we may always appeal to it; Job is justified by ethics alone. Virtue creates concord in the soul, and the good man cannot be harmed; he can find happiness even in the burning Bull of Phalaris. And if the virtuous man should live to witness not himself but his children led into the ovens at Dachau, we shall say to him, weep not, curse nothing, but understand.

On Socrates' view, however, the abyss and therefore the God relationship are out of the picture completely, as is the single individual. If it should be objected that virtue is a gift of God, we may reply that once we have the gift, we no longer need God—we become as the gods. Indeed, the deception of virtue has already been brought out; the ethical is not the gift of God but the temptation of the serpent. Once the ethical is perceived through new eyes as a temptation and is thus pulled out from under him, the individual is thrown back upon himself and discovers the abyss. He is now faced with making the leap that will carry him over the abyss into a relationship with God in which all things are possible.

In the movement toward the second dimension of thought, as in the movement of faith, the first thing the individual must oppose is the ethical. Insofar as both the rational and the ethical demand ubiquity, the one is inextricably bound to the other; both function on the basis of the precepts embodied by the Tree of Knowledge. Reason, says Shestov, seeks mechanical explanations; in the moral world it is justice, in the material world balance (J, 59). Thus in his book on Tolstoy and Nietzsche Shestov objects to Tolstoy's identification of God with the Good. Rather, he supports Nietzsche's claim that "God is the Good" and "God is dead" amount to the same thing.[57] God, who is beyond necessity, is without conceptual direction, without the signposts of good and evil. The ethical, however, operates within a system and seeks a necessary imperative for direction no less than the rational; it is maintained solely by its connection with necessity and its universal application. When the religious comes up against the ethical there arises in the first instance a dread of itself disappearing into the ethical. In order to keep from losing his religious stance so that he may ascend and return from Moriah, the individual must make the movement of resignation and decisively suspend the ethical. Here the ethical no longer leads us away from ourselves because it is no longer cast in the mold of necessity; it has been qualified by the passionate and personal God relationship.

In Abraham we have already seen the depth of the opposition of faith and morality and the nameless agony in which the movement of faith must be made. Where Jesus passed a single night in Gethsemane in dread of the trial awaiting him, what shall we add to the dread of Abraham, who in his trial spent three nights in the wilderness alongside his son who was to die under his knife? Like the underground man, Abraham discovered that contrary to the Catholic declaration that God does not demand the impossible, God does indeed demand the impossible; God demands nothing but the impossible, or perhaps better, God demands nothing but the unthinkable. Because in Abraham's case the ethical has presented itself as a temptation, we require a second dimension of thought in order to "understand" him. For Abraham is not like the tragic hero, whose dilemma can be mediated in the ethical—once justice is served, harmony and balance are restored. With Abraham, however, the restoration of harmony begins the trial anew.

Shestov asserts that in the end ethics reveals to us the nothingness of all that is of this world (J, 353). The problem of evil, for example, or the difficulty which led Ivan Karamazov to return his "ticket," is born of the ethical. But, again, such a revelation

74

comes upon us only when the ethical collides with the religious, when both bring to bear the sum of their import. One way to avoid the conflict is to seek a neutral ground. For Abraham, the emptiness as well as the sheer weight of the ethical in the face of the sacrifice led him to infinitely resign himself to God's will and the loss of Isaac. The state of resignation may look very much like the piety and obedience which Spinoza ascribed to faith; indeed, reason can have no other description of faith. But when faith is rendered in terms of resignation alone, it is neither the passion nor the paradox that Kierkegaard and Shestov understand it to be. For in the state of resignation the individual continues to be understood in terms of the ethical, since it is in the light of the ethical that he has resigned himself: I must murder my son, he is forever lost—there is no helping it. The man in resignation still has his attention focused on the finite self, on the obedient "I" as subject to God's will, and not on the lost, eternal self which seeks a personal relation to God. Here the individual remains within the nothingness and necessity of the world and has stopped at that. Hence in order to make the movement of faith, something more than infinite resignation and a suspension of the ethical is required.

There is nothing in the mechanics of the sacrifice itself which would make it a sacrifice rather than a murder. What we think of as the reality of the deed belongs to the universal, to the language of the rational and the ethical, where Abraham is a murderer, Job's children are lost and Jesus lies dead and buried. Whether the act is carried out in resignation or in faith, the objective description of it remains the same. Thus it is not the act which Abraham performs that is of interest but rather what happens to him in the performance of it; the significance of the trial lies within. This is why the paradox of faith may be expressed by saying the internal is superior to the external; the lamentation, which is turned inward, toward the soul, is superior to the understanding, which is turned outward, toward individual objects, and strives to silence lamentation.

The second dimension of thought, then, is directed inward; its task is to internalize. It is subjective, concentrating on the inward life of the thinking subject; for the second dimension of thought, the internal is superior to the external. Perhaps we may now see in what sense the sufferings of Job weigh heavier than the

75

sand of the sea, heavier than the external reality with
all its necessary and universal truths. Whereas the
universal nature of the rational and the ethical provides us with direction, there is no direction for the
man who seeks with lamentation, and he cannot make himself understood. Like Abraham raising his knife over
his son, he cannot state his case without losing his
case and must set out without knowing where he is going.
This is what so amazed Shestov about Tolstoy's departure from home one night in 1910:

> He grew sick of all his achievements,
> all his glory. Everything grew heavy,
> agonizing, unbearable. It is as if he
> tears his venerability away from himself
> with a trembling and impatient hand. . .
> along with all the symbols of his wisdom
> and status as a teacher, in order to
> stand before the final Judgement with a
> light, or at least a lighter soul; he
> was compelled to forget and renounce the
> sum of his great past (J, 139).

Thus everything must be sacrificed for nothing.

Finally, it must be asked why Shestov calls the
second dimension a dimension of <u>thought</u> when he sees it
as something which is beyond language. Might it not be
considered as something other than thought? We have
seen that speculative thought is indifferent to the existence of the thinking subject. Its object is to relate the individual to truth, where the attention is
focused on whether or not the thing related to is indeed the truth; its emphasis is on the outcome rather
than the process, on the being rather than the becoming,
and it proceeds from the individual outward. The second
dimension of thought, however, puts everything into a
process of becoming and omits the outcome. It proceeds
from the subject inward, where the emphasis is not on
the content of thought as such but on what happens to
the individual while thinking. Under the second dimension of thought, for example, reflection is not concerned with the problem of whether its object is the
true God but whether the individual is related to the
object in such a way that the relationship is truly a
God relationship. Because the second dimension of
thought is thus rooted in inwardness, it culminates in
the passion of the individual and not in the language
of the world. And passion finds its expression in paradox: if my grief were laid in the balances it would

weigh heavier than the sand of the sea.

Since speculative thought cannot bring us to the second dimension of thought, we can only break through with a leap, an infinite movement, which must be effected by passion. Yet the passion launching us into the second dimension cannot be distinguished from it, so that it appears to be a passion and not a dimension of thought after all. In terms of Shestov's biblical philosophy, it is the passion of faith, and the temptation that would prevent the movement of faith is that of reason, ethics and natural necessity—the temptation of the serpent. Thus in the passion of faith, where thought leaves off, Job came to declare, "Though after my skin worms destroy this body, yet in my flesh shall I see God: Whom I shall see for myself, and mine eyes shall behold, and not another; though my reins be consumed within me" (Job 19:27-28).

## NOTES

1. Nikolai Berdyaev, The Russian Idea (New York: MacMillan, 1948), p. 235.
2. Berdyaev, introduction to Lev Shestov, Umozrenie i otkrovenie (Paris: YMCA Press, 1964), pp. 5-6.
3. Albert Camus, Le mythe de Sisyphe (Paris: Gallimard, 1942), p. 42.
4. Ibid., pp. 41-42.
5. V. V. Zenkovsky, A History of Russian Philosophy, Vol. 2, tr. George L. Kline (London: Routledge & Kegan Paul, 1953), p. 782.
6. Ibid., pp. 790-791.
7. Ibid., p. 783.
8. Ibid., p. 784.
9. Lev Shestov, "Dnevnik myslei," Kontinent, 8 (1978), 252.
10. Zenkovsky, History, p. 789.
11. Bernard Martin, introduction to Shestov, In Job's Balances, tr. Camilla Coventry and C. A. Macartney (Athens: Ohio University Press, 1975), p. xvii.
12. Ibid., p. xviii.
13. Ibid., p. xxvii.
14. Soren Kierkegaard, Repetition, tr. Walter Lowrie (Princeton: Princeton University Press, 1941), p. 130.
15. Shestov, Umozrenie, pp. 211-212.
16. Immanuel Kant, Ueber das Misslingen aller philosophischen Versuche in der Theodicee in Sämtliche Werke, Vol. 4 (Leipzig: Inselverlag, 1921), pp. 810-813.
17. Kierkegaard, Repetition, pp. 130-133-

18. Shestov, Na vesakh Iova (Paris: La societe nouvelle d'Éditions Franco-Slaves, 1929), p. 29. All further references to this work will be followed by the letter "J" and page number.
19. F. M. Dostoevsky, Zapiski iz mĕrtvogo doma in Sobranie sochinenii, Vol. 3 (Moscow, 1958), p. 577.
20. Dostoevsky, Zapiski iz podpol'ya, SS, Vol. 4, p. 133.
21. Shestov, Dostoevsky i Nietzsche—Filosofiya tragedii, 4th Ed. (Paris: YMCA Press, 1971), p. 51.
22. Shestov, Afiny i Ierusalim (Paris: YMCA Press, 1951), p. 147.
23. Dostoevsky, Idiot, SS, Vol. 6, p. 26.
24. Ibid., p. 76.
25. Anna Dostoevskaya, Reminiscences, tr. Beatrice Stillman (New York: Liveright, 1977), pp. 21-22.
26. Shestov, Afiny, p. 149.
27. Shestov, Umozrenie, p. 87.
28. Shestov, Kierkegaard and the Existential Philosophy, tr. Elinor Hewitt (Athens: Ohio University Press, 1969), p. 108.
29. L. N. Tolstoy, Polse bala in Sobranie sochinenii, Vol. 14 (Moscow, 1964), p. 16.
30. Shestov, Umozrenie, p. 159.
31. Shestov, Afiny, p. 47.
32. Tolstoy, Smert' Ivana Il'icha, SS, Vol. 12, p. 92.
33. Ibid., p. 94.
34. Tolstoy, Khozyain i rabotnik, SS, Vol. 12, p. 364.
35. Dostoevsky, Son smeshnogo cheloveka, SS, Vol. 10, p. 437.
36. Shestov, "Dnevnik," 251.
37. Benedict de Spinoza, Tractatus Politicus in Opera, Vol. 2, 3rd Ed. (The Hague: Martin Nijhoff, 1914), p. 4.
38. Blaise Pascal, Pensées (Paris: Club des Libraires de France, 1961), p. 240.
39. Spinoza, Ethics, tr. William Hale White, revised Amelia Hutchinson Stirling, ed. James Gutmann (New Tork: Hafner Publishing Co., 1949), p. 269.
40. Ibid., p. 187.
41. Ibid., p. 280.
42. Shestov, Afiny, p. 110.
43. Pascal, Pensées, p. 21.
44. Spinoza, Ethics, p. 115.
45. Shestov, Umozrenie, pp. 45-46.
46. Thorleif Boman, Hebrew Thought Compared with Greek, tr. James L. Moreau (New York: W. W. Norton, 1960), p. 201.

47. Pascal, Pensées, p. 245.
48. Shestov, Potestas Clavium, tr. Bernard Martin (Athens: Ohio University Press, 1968), p. 111.
49. Karl Jaspers, Die grossen Philosophen, Vol. 1 (Munich: R. Piper, 1957), p. 664.
50. Plotinus, Enneads, Vol. 3, tr. A. H. Armstrong (Cambridge: Harvard University Press, 1966), p. 391.
51. Jaspers, Philosophen, p. 666.
52. Shestov, Afiny, p. 191.
53. Shestov, Kierkegaard, p. 27.
54. Boman, Thought, p. 27.
55. Erich Auerbach, Mimesis (Bern: A. Francke AG, 1946), p. 16.
56. Shestov, Afiny, p. 15.
57. Shestov, Dobro v uchenii gr. Tolstogo i F. Nietzsche, 5th Ed. (Paris: YMCA Press, 1971), pp. 96-100.

ESSAY III

## FAITH, PHILOSOPHY AND
## LITERATURE: SHESTOV AND DOSTOEVSKY

Shestov was a philosopher whose profound concern with faith led him to explore the passionate outcries of literature as well as the labyrinthine ruminations of philosophy. Like Kierkegaard, his thinking is as much lyrical as it is dialectical, and he turned to those literary figures whose art is as much dialectical as it is lyrical. For the "second dimension of thought" or the dimension of faith is not peculiar to philosophy. It has a tinge of the artistic about it and is always closely alligned with literary endeavor. Indeed, when faith is an issue, philosophy and literature are of a piece, since here both are concerned not with universal principles or categorical imperatives but with the passion and the outcry of a Job or a Karamazov. In this essay, then, I shall examine Shestov's approach to Dostoevsky in order to see how and why the "ordinary" disciplinary distinctions between philosophy and literature collapse when faith is in question. Here there is no philosophy, no literature, just outcry.

In his book on literature and philosophy Stephen Ross explains the difference between the two by saying that according to one tradition, literature may either demonstrate philosophical positions, or it may adopt and make claims about them, or it may do both.[1] Ross goes on to assert that literature has a "fundamental contribution to make that is difficult for science and philosophy to offer consistently—that of revealing the irrational, the horrible, or the obvious."[2] When he uses the word "philosophy," however, he refers to what Shestov calls speculative or theoretical philosophy. It is difficult for speculative philosophy to unearth the terrors or the absurd in life precisely because it strives to do away with a passionate, as opposed to a rational, reaction to the horrible. On Ross's view, literature may add something to the thought process which speculative philosophy does not provide, but the one is not necessarily in conflict with the other, and both retain their disciplinary separation.

Such a position is not very far removed from that of Julian Ross, who maintains that literature may be of assistance to philosophy insofar as it expresses an abstract idea in terms of "the concrete person and event."[3] Expanding on this, he explains,

81

> Intuitive perception, when organized and
> controlled in a work of art, is not hos-
> tile but complementary to pure logic, and
> can relate ideas which logic alone is in-
> capable of expressing. Literature, then,
> has the power not only to illustrate the
> concepts of philosophy, but to bring about
> a mood of imaginative understanding which
> carries them alive into the minds and emo-
> tions of its readers.[4]

Once again the word "philosophy" is used to mean speculative philosophy, philosophy governed by logic and the
law of contradiction. Like Stephen Ross, Julian Ross
sees the basic distinction between literature and philosophy as a distinction between the emotional and the
rational faculties. In both cases literature provides a
complement, though not a necessary one, to speculative
philosophy in that the particular and emotional concerns of literature may reveal something of interest
about the general and rational concerns of philosophy.

Because Shestov is involved in existential philosophy, however, he has removed the focus of philosophy
from the universal to the individual who must enact the
drama of living and dying; existential philosophy proceeds from the single individual to the universal and
not the other way around. Here the individual is in a
sense superior to the universal; for Shestov, as well
as for Dostoevsky, there can be no abstract idea apart
from the living individual. Therefore the relationship
between philosophy and literature as revealed by a comparison of Dostoevsky and Shestov must differ funda-
mentally from the connection between philosophy and
literature conceived by Stephen Ross and Julian Ross.
Existential philosophy and literature stand in a relation which is unifying rather than complementary; where
existential thought is of interest, the literature assumes the aspects of the philosophy and the philosophy
the aspects of the literature.

In their literary and philosophical endeavors Dostoevsky and Shestov develop a concept of faith which
lies beyond the limits of speculation and rests on the
absurd, so that they are of a piece in their efforts to
begin where thought leaves off. In the transformation
of thought that comes about in the attempt to give
voice to the unspeakable, the disciplinary distinctions
between philosophy and literature are no longer significant, since it is speculative thought that creates the

distinctions and divides knowledge into separate categories or departments. The question of what happens to the individual in giving voice to his faith and his existence takes precedence over the form and content of thought, and those who are set on maintaining the separation of the disciplines have failed to comprehend this important aspect of existentialism. Here existential thought may be termed religious thought, since it is characterized by paradox and contradiction—in my flesh shall I see God, though my reins be consumed within me.

Thus we have a transformation of thought that comes about in the attempt to speak the unspeakable. In Shestov's approach to Dostoevsky there are in fact four elements of this transformation which unify their philosophy and literature: (1) the self in contemplation of itself, (2) the unattainable possibility, (3) the expression of possibility and (4) the transformation of thought itself. Here lies the key to understanding the unity of existential philosophy and literature as it comes out in Shestov's treatment of Dostoevsky, a unity which rests on the common concern of faith.

### 1. The Self in Contemplation of Itself

In matters of faith there is an emphasis on inwardness, an insistence upon the importance of being inner-directed. In order to make sense of being inner-directed we must first consider that empirical or outward aspect of ourselves which is part of the material continuum of the world. Each of us forms what physicists call a world-line; each of us is a unit of matter in a temporal progression through space. Physicists have further taught us that we can speak of a spatio-temporal existence only in terms of matter or energy, yet we seem to approach and speak of existence from somewhere else, from "outside." We are not simply matter or a biological complex of chemical reactions: we are matter <u>aware</u> of itself and its existence, conscious of its life and death.

Although our empirical or physical aspect is part of the physical world, consciousness places the world "out there" all around us and brings us before the world. Consciousness is not confined to the immediate in the way the empirical is: it extends itself spatially toward the infinitely large and the infinitely small. It dwells on the comparative—bigger, farther, smaller, smaller still. It extends itself in time toward the remote past and the distant future, into its own past and future, but it can never contain all of space and time, for consciousness observes in its future, as well as in its past, a nothingness that borders it. In the past it is birth, in the future death; time is a prison. Although consciousness may for the present move beyond its birth and death, in the present it is aware of a time in the future when it will no longer be aware of anything; both the empirical and the conscious aspects of the individual will dissolve. The individual must remain separate from and contained within the universal, subject to the laws that rule the physical world.

As consciousness exerts itself through the will to extend or expand itself, there emerges a longing to contain that by which it is contained. The unit of matter or the empirical self cannot encompass; it is enclosed, a horizon within a greater horizon, constantly consuming the fruits of the physical world only to be consumed by the laws, by the stone wall, of the physical world. Because the flesh-and-blood self is enclosed, it is determined from the outside and cannot be self-sustaining. Matter aware of itself is aware of the enclosure and the death of the empirical self. But since the awareness is itself enclosing, it strives to enclose rather than be enclosed, for only that which is all-encompassing can be absolutely self-sustaining and therefore authentically self-authored. Thus the longing to encompass directs the drive toward authenticity inward, where all that is without is subjectively internalized in a process of fusion and reconstruction. Witness Goethe's Faust, for example, the man who longed to know everything knowledge could offer, to suffer all sufferings, to enjoy all joys, to internalize and appropriate the sum of existence.

It is the longing to encompass, and not simply consciousness, that creates a sense of spiritual self, a self that might be sold to a Mephistopheles. The self in contemplation of itself expresses its will to be in its will to encompass; it longs not simply to exist but to be existence. For a moment, says Nietzsche, we become that Primal Being and experience its hunger for existence, the necessity of the torment, and the pain of the destruction of appearances.[5]

Because the self strives to encompass the totality and thereby achieve authenticity, the self may be described as this very longing to be existence. But the self that wills to be what it is not is a divided self,

a self in discord with itself. There is the encompassing existence which the self longs to be set against
the encompassed existence which characterizes the longing. Because there is a spiritual aspect of the self,
it cannot absorb the less-than-total; for the individual who longs to encompass, the encompassed self is no
self.

To borrow from the language of Kierkegaard, the
self in its longing is suspended at the critical zero
point, between something and nothing, a mere Perhaps.
Here nothingness assumes the features of something more
than blank nothingness: it becomes the Other within,
the devouring complement to the Perhaps, and this is
what gives weight to the question that issues from the
Perhaps. The revelations found in Notes from Underground, says Shestov, do not come in the form of answers but in the form of questions.[6] Yet they are not
questions that can be answered, and reason therefore
declares that they are not questions at all. Indeed,
reason refuses to acknowledge revelation altogether,
since it does not follow from existing premises; it can
neither be collected nor recollected. Shestov explains,

> When reason grows weak, when truth dies,
> when the light goes out—only then do
> the words of Revelation become accessible
> to man. And, conversely, as long as we
> have the light, reason and truth, we
> drive Revelation away from ourselves.[7]

Hence Dostoevsky has Ippolit meet Myshkin in The Idiot
only to ridicule Myshkin in the face of Ippolit's question of how to die a decent death.[8] But Myshkin does
not deem the question foolish or unintelligible: he
answers it—pass us by and forgive us our happiness—
even though he knows full well the impotence of any
reply.

Ippolit places Myshkin before the stone wall of
Notes from Underground, where we read,

> These gentlemen in certain circumstances
> may bellow like bulls at the top of their
> lungs, and let's assume this brings them
> the greatest honor. But as I have already
> said, in the face of the impossible they
> immediately fall silent. The impossible
> means the stone wall! Which stone wall?
> Why it goes without saying, the laws of

nature, the conclusions of natural
science, mathematics.[9]

The Angel of Death opens our eyes to death as a ruling,
indifferent and unassailable law of existence, and we
ourselves are the evidence that proves the law. More
than that, we have constructed the wall stone by tablet
of stone, using the mortar of reason, ethics and natural necessity; we have fixed the expression and in so
doing have paralyzed the voice.

Once the collision with the stone wall is internalized, the self which is aware of the presence of the
Other as the void within encounters its own end. The
point of the question raised by Ippolit and the underground man is not to reveal a fear of what will happen
to all of us but to bring out the terror of a condition
in which the self must inevitably disappear into the
Other. For an instant the severed head sees the box
rushing toward itself, and the thud of its falling into
the box reveals the horror of the box, of irretrievable
enclosure. Being faced with the encompassing impossibility further reinforces the longing to encompass. The
something begins to push against the nothing, and as it
does, the self gains strength for its struggle with the
unattainable possibility.

## 2. The Unattainable Possibility

Shestov's interest in Ippolit and the underground
man lies in the fact that for them death or nothingness
has made a genuinely concernful existence impossible.
In despair the individual wills both to be and not to
be himself; he flees from a state of being characterized by impossibility but at the same time hopes to
somehow attain that unattainable possibility. As for so
many of Dostoevsky's literary characters, this is the
drive behind Shestov's philosophy.

In order to acquire a better feel for the weight
of the silence created by the questions of despair, we
would do well to take one more quote from Dostoevsky,
this time from the words of Kirillov in The Demons:

> Listen to a great idea: there was one day
> in this world when three crosses stood
> at the center of the earth. One of the
> men on a cross had such faith that he
> had said to another, 'Today you will be
> with me in paradise.' The day ended,

86

both died, passed away, and found
neither paradise nor resurrection.
What was said did not come true. Listen: this man was the loftiest on all
the earth; He gave meaning to life.
The whole planet, with everything on
it, is nothing but madness without that
man. Neither before nor since has there
ever been another like Him. And if this
is so, if the laws of nature did not
spare even Him, did not spare even their
miracle, but made Him live in a lie and
die in a lie, then the whole planet is
a lie and rests on a lie and a stupid
mockery. Thus the very laws of this
world are a lie and a vaudeville of
demons. What is there to live for?
Answer if you're a man![10]

Kirillov is an individual who in despair wills
both to be and not to be himself. His life has come to
a stop; God has been lost at Golgotha and with Him all
possibility of authenticity. "God is necessary and
therefore He must exist," says Kirillov. "But I know He
does not and cannot exist. . . . Surely you understand
that one may shoot oneself because of this alone."[11]
This is the torment Shestov speaks of when he tells us,
"All the heroes of The Demons—not only Kirillov and
Shatov but Stavrogin too—in the end tell the tale of
how Dostoevsky, like Dmitri Karamazov, was tormented
all his life by God."[12]

Resolved to take his own life, Kirillov flees from
a condition characterized by the impossibility of authentic existence, yet at the same time he hopes somehow to attain this unattainable possibility. Suicide
appears as the only hope, as the one means of encompassing, but the encompassing comes at the expense of
any consciousness of it, and the individual is again
thrown back on the void and the pain of staring it in
the face. For the self can never encompass as long as
it is divided in its desire to encompass; the very desire precludes the encompassing. The destruction of the
longing opens the way to the unattainable possibility
of encompassing, and the temptation of suicide becomes
still more compelling. Thus Kirillov declares, "He who
kills himself in order to kill fear will immediately
become God."[13]

Given that God might be described as the condition

in which all things are possible, a condition contained neither by the laws of nature nor by the dictates of reason, the movement toward the unattainable possibility is a movement toward the God relationship. In suicide the self responds to nothingness by plunging into it rather than synthesizing it with itself. When the self disappears into this Other, it does just that—it disappears. The Other is no longer Other, the self no longer self; and when the self is lost, the God relationship is lost. Since it is this world, this life, that must be regained, suicide can only be a false solution. An alternative must be found, and this returns the individual to the critical zero point, to the Perhaps, which is forever finished but never fulfilled.

In Dostoevsky's literary expression despair and suicide follow the encounter with death in a chronological order; Kirillov's temptation to suicide and his ultimate submission to that temptation have their chronological coordinates. In Shestov's philosophical expression despair and its prospect of suicide as both a movement toward God and a judgement of God set the stage for a Last Judgement of both man and God. The outcome of the Judgement hangs on the precarious Perhaps, and the Perhaps lies outside any temporal coordinate system; as indicated above, it is marked by "forever" and "never." Shestov's emphasis is not on the event or the act of suicide so much as on its implications for a Last Judgement.

The individual confronts himself in such a way that he must qualitatively measure himself, and this implies judgement. The implications of suicide for the instant make the instant one of judgement, so that the eternity of the judgement is contained in the temporality of the instant. The philosophical and literary modes of expression are unified in their conjunction of the temporal and the eternal, and whatever may be said about genre, style, structure or aesthetic balance in connection with Dostoevsky, his work cannot be properly understood as existential literature until one draws on existential philosophy as Shestov has done. Both Dostoevsky and Shestov bring out the gravity of the instant not only as a particle of time but as "the finite reflection of eternity in time, its first effort as it were to bring time to a stop."[14]

When the longing to encompass is destroyed in the act of suicide it may seem that eternity is gained, but because time is lost, so too is eternity. The struggle

for the unattainable possibility is not a struggle to
replace time with eternity but to join the two; it is a
struggle for the absurd possibility that time and eternity are inseparable. Once the instant of judgement has
been internalized, the individual moves into a life in
time that is qualified by a life in eternity, a life
before God. Thus the problem for existential thought is
now to express the eternal in terms of the historical,
so that the individual existing in the historical may
encompass from within and thus attain a kind of salvation. Here, again, the individual is superior to the
universal.

Describing the task of existential thought in this
way, one may see why Kierkegaard took it to be so
closely tied to Christianity as the one instance of the
eternal resting on and reflected in the historical:

> It is well known that Christianity is the
> only historical phenomenon which in spite
> of the historical, nay precisely by means
> of the historical, has offered itself to
> the individual as a point of departure
> for his eternal consciousness, has as-
> sumed to interest him in another sense
> than the merely historical, has proposed
> to base his eternal happiness on his re-
> lationship to something historical. No
> system of philosophy, addressing itself
> only to thought, no mythology, addressing
> itself solely to the imagination, no his-
> torical knowledge, addressing itself to
> memory, has ever had this idea.[15]

The idea to which Kierkegaard refers presents itself as
the Perhaps externalized; expression becomes an alternative to disappearing into the Other. But when expression addresses itself solely to thought, imagination or
memory (recollection), it founders on contradiction and
paradox, so that existential expression must try to
take up where thought leaves off, and in its attempt to
do so it must undergo a transformation of thought. We
must embrace the paradox and set out without knowing
where we go, for as soon as we have the moment as an
atom of eternity, we have the paradox. The struggle for
the unattainable possibility therefore becomes a struggle for the expression of possibility, and this is
characteristic of existential expression. Existential
literature does not seek to express truth, beauty, virtue, reality or the sublime, as other literary forms

have been said to do; rather, it seeks the expression of possibility, and Shestov and Dostoevsky show us that in the struggle for expression existential philosophy and literature are of a piece.

### 3. The Expression of Possibility

The word implies not only the existence of another to whom it is uttered but a division within the speaker himself and an attempt at the dialectical synthesis which may close the division. Both the literary endeavor of Dostoevsky and the philosophical effort of Shestov constitute a struggle for the expression of possibility through the word; it is a seeking for a voice by means of which the self may call to and bridge with the Other which is itself. Here the unity of existential philosophy and literature grows somewhat more visible, since both stand in the same context of self-creation, the context of presence and absence, of self calling to Other. In the first instance it is the context of the lama sabachthani uttered at the stone wall, and this too is characteristic of existential expression.

Although the voice which issues from the divided self arises in an attempt to heal the division, existential expression is not to be taken as an expression of truth. Truth as the revelation of the synthesized whole cannot be communicated because it is undivided and without opposition. We may glimpse the truth or the mystery, says Shestov, but we cannot communicate it; we cannot make it universal and necessary. When we try, we begin to see as the world sees and to speak as it demands (J, 81). Since the word implies division seeking union, existential expression takes the form of a question which has no answer other than one of contradiction and paradox. In the existential expression of possibility, possibility is attained by passionately sustaining the question and with it the paradox.

Given that language normally functions on a rational level, according to intelligible rules, the expression of possibility is a means of articulating the paradox of the historicity of the eternal reflected in the instant, so that the paradox is not lost to language but is regained through probing the limits of language by means of language itself. When language is stretched in this way it becomes more artistic, more poetic: it is a literary process. The poet plays with the language, but in this case the impetus to probe the word has its origin in and cannot be separated from a

90

philosophical difficulty.

Genuine existence lies in the expression of possibility. Existential literature takes its approach from the event and the experience, the way of life embodied by the word; existential philosophy proceeds from the contemplation of the passion itself and its ramifications for a way of life. Although each thinker sets out from a different direction, the point of reference, the subjective existence of the single individual, is the same.

As an expression of possibility, the word provides an occasion for the attempt on the part of consciousness to shape reality. The need to do so, however, does not arise until a previous reality falls apart and the ground crumbles from under our feet. When this occurs the self that had been steeped in an illusory reality witnesses the dissolution of itself. As Shestov has indicated, this is what happens when Dostoevsky's underground man discovers that "twice two is four" is a principle of death (J, 56). Such is the equation, the balance of reason and ethics, acquired in the consumption of the Fruit from the Tree of Knowledge, and, says Shestov, the question raised by Dostoevsky's Grand Inquisitor is whether or not the serpent was a deceiver (J, 87). Thus the question of shaping reality through the expression of possibility arises only after the forbidden Fruit has been eaten and the individual has discovered that the Tree of Knowledge is not the Tree of Life. The hand that reaches for the Fruit is the hand that refuses to be drained of life. The Fruit is devoured, we see the life draining, and more desperately than ever we refuse.

Shestov believed that one major aim of Dostoevsky's efforts was to try to understand the Fall (J, 80). Recall, for example, The Dream of the Ridiculous Man. As Berdyaev put it, on Shestov's view, "the Fall was not ontological but gnosiological; it was due to the rise of the knowledge of good and evil, that is to say, the rise of the generally and universally obligatory, the necessary."[16] The Fall is gnosiological rather than ontological because the rise of knowledge does not in fact alter or reign over existence—it diverts us away from authentic existence and traps us in the net of reflection. The fallen individual is like a man with a wooden leg: he cannot take a step without reflection, without looking to see where he is headed.

91

The temptation of the serpent, of the Grand Inquisitor, is to allow ourselves to be shaped by necessity so that we will not have to assume the task of freely creating ourselves. But this is precisely the task we must take up in the expression of possibility. The voice that calls out to its Other in an effort to achieve a synthesis with the Other calls out to itself, to what it shall have been by virtue of what it is coming to be. As the shaping agent, the self becomes the voice in the whirlwind by placing itself in the whirlwind, in the chaos, and chaos, Shestov points out, "is not limited possibility, but on the contrary, it is unlimited possibility" (J, 215). Thus the self emerges as the creator, as the fiat creating through expression. Reality is no longer the occasion or material for the word but is rather molded by means of the word in such a way that the existence of the genuine self is held in a moving dialectic, suspended over the abyss.

If consciousness is encompassed or limited by thought, so too is the self, which means that the self cannot be self-sustaining, and therefore it cannot be authentic. It is in the confines of thought, then, that the self encounters the stone wall or the impossible which induces the desire for the unattainable, unthinkable possibility. The expression of possibility comes about in an attempt to encompass thought, or rather to move beyond thought, where "reality" does not shape the self in thought but instead is shaped by the self in a transformation of thought, that is, in an alteration of the categories that govern thought. That which is eternal, for example, no longer lies outside the category of that which is historical; that which is mortal no longer lies outside the category of that which is immortal. Such an alteration of the categories we employ in our thinking requires a change in the nature of thought itself. What is necessary no longer need be accepted just because it is necessary, and contradiction no longer implies error or falsehood. The reality so created by the authentic self is what Shestov calls the "genuine reality" when he says,

> As the soul nears the genuine reality, terror overwhelms it; it feels as if it were beign submerged into nothingness, as if it were perishing. And when we try to capture the ultimate, higher reality in the fine and well-formulated nets of the categories we have prepared and are used to, that reality eludes

them like water running through fish
nets (J, 307-308).

Thus in order to gain the authentic self in the shaping
of a genuine reality, the expression of possibility
which renders the unattainable attainable can only take
place in a transformation of the categories.

## 4. The Transformation of Thought

The attainment of possibility through expression
comes in a transformation of thought, and when thought
is transformed, so is the self and the reality it
shapes. In the metamorphosis the self nears the "higher
reality" and indeed feels as if it were perishing, for
it is born anew in a creation of itself from the ashes
of itself. The self-creation of self is the impossible
alternative to a self-inflicted fading into nothingness,
yet in a sense it is precisely by fading into the void,
without knowing where we are going, that the authentic
self is created; the individual becomes independent of
the universality of rational and ethical truths by
being reduced to nothing before God. This is the "something more" that Shestov and Dostoevsky are struggling
for. It is the hope that the self might become something more by virtue of having been reduced to nothing,
the hope that there might occur a repetition of the
self in such a way that everything begins and nothing
ends. Existence is the opposite of finality.

The self as the agent of creation is a self in the
process of becoming, and the fear and trembling which
overshadow this self-creation are the signifiers of becoming. In the language of Kierkegaard, the transformation of thought is characterized by the shift from objective to subjective thought. Kierkegaard correctly
observes that "whenever the subjective is of importance
in knowledge, and where appropriation thus constitutes
the crux of the matter, the process of communication is
a work of art, and doubly reflected."[17] Both for Shestov and for Dostoevsky expression is doubly reflected
because the self is both the agent and the subject of
creation; the self both participates and observes.

In Shestov's treatment of Dostoevsky we find a
philosophical difficulty dealt with by taking a literary
mode of expression as a point of departure. Although the
philosophy and the literature are distinguishable from
each other, the one must be understood in terms of the
other, just as valleys must be understood in terms of

mountains. In regard to the philosophy as well as the literature, the truth of existential expression cannot be measured according to its conformity with reason or with empirical "fact" but is rather determined according to the possibility which it reveals for the existence of the single individual; the static categories of the intellect must be displaced by the dynamic going forth of the passion.

The significance of the transformation of thought for existential philosophy and literature is that it unites one mode with the other. For Shestov, the word becomes a means of creation or revelation, a means to possibility, rather than a building block in a system erected on necessity; his philosophy thus becomes literary, artistic. Zenkovsky says of Shestov in this connection,

> Shestov impresses one with his extra-
> ordinary literary talent. He not only
> writes attractively and clearly; he
> moves the reader by a simplicity rare
> in a writer, and by an absence of all
> affectation and pursuit of 'style.'
> Shestov somehow combines elegance and
> power of expression with a rigour and
> purity of verbal form. The result is an
> irresistable impression of authenticity
> and honesty. It may be that these quali-
> ties of Shestov's writing have been the
> reason why literary circles have valued,
> and continue to value him much more
> highly than philosophical circles. How-
> ever, the basic inspiration of Shestov's
> work is philosophic.[18]

Existential philosophy as represented by Shestov may be described as what Stephen Ross calls a "basically artistic medium" when he says, "If the rational tradition is on the wrong track, only a basically artistic medium can represent that fact."[19]

In his Dictionary of Literary Terms Henry Shaw defines existential writing as "writing that emphasizes man's responsibility for forming his own nature and that stresses the prime importance of personal decisions, personal freedom, and personal goals."[20] He states further that

> . . . existentialists are (1) concerned

94

with man's essential being and nature,
(2) convinced that thought and reason
are insufficient to understand and cope
with the mysteries of living, (3) conscious that anguish and despair are the
common lot of everyone, and (4) fixed
in the belief that a sense of morality
depends upon positive and active par-
ticipation in life.[21]

In their Dictionary of Literary, Dramatic, and Cinematic Terms Barnet, Berman and Burto explain,

The philosophical and literary writings
of existentialists stress the insecurity,
loneliness, and irrevocability of man's
experience; the perilous situations in
which these characteristics are most
salient; and the serious, involved, and
anxious striving of responsible men to
face the situations, or the evasive,
desperate, and ultimately futile attempts
of weak men to escape them.[22]

When literature becomes existential its task is no longer that of arousing certain emotions, teaching virtue,
reflecting reality, transmitting feelings or even dis-
playing philosophical ideas. Instead, like existential
philosophy, existential literature seeks possibility
in a transformation of thought; it is doubly reflected
and thus shapes itself and a new reality, as opposed to
being shaped by and conforming to a standing reality.

The significance of existential expression, whether it takes the form of philosophy or literature, does
not lie in its content as such but, again, in what hap-
pans to us in the implementation and internalization of
expression. The interest is in the passion by virtue of
which the transformation of thought is effected; and
because the transformation comes in a leap, the passion
is precisely the passion of faith. Since the emphasis
on the content of thought has been removed, faith cannot be characterized by a belief in God or the acceptance of religious teachings, and the distinction between theistic and atheistic existentialism is a false
and misleading one. The so-called theistic and atheistic versions of existentialism are both focused on the
self as Perhaps opposite the self as Other; both are
primarily concerned with the task of self-creation in
the expression of possibility. In short, the attention

95

of both is on the movement of faith as a passionate
struggle for possibility. This is what Shestov has in
mind when he says, "Existential philosophy, which is so
closely united with faith that only in the presence of
and through faith can it do its work, finds in faith
that new dimension which sets it apart from theoretical
philosophy."[23] Dostoevsky's relationship to his literary work may be rendered in the same terms. In Shestov's approach to Dostoevsky we discover therefore that
existential philosophy and literature are united in the
transformation of thought which occurs in the movement
of faith.

Thus we see the unity of existential philosophy
and literature as revealed by Shestov's approach to
Dostoevsky. Both proceed toward the same passionate and
personal metamorphosis. And since that which proceeds
in passion must be comprehended in passion, the philosophical and literary modes of expression require one
and the same mode of comprehension. Once the transformation of thought begins to take form in expression, we
must find the courage to receive what is said as if it
were the issue of an inner voice. We must seek our own
existential possibility in such a way that the lama
sabachthani of a Dostoevsky becomes our own, just as it
became Shestov's own.

## NOTES

1. Stephen D. Ross, Literature and Philosophy (New
York: Appleton-Century-Crofts, 1969), p. 3.
2. Ibid., p. 56.
3. Julian L. Ross, Philosophy in Literature (Syracuse: Syracuse University Press, 1949), p. 134.
4. Ibid., p. 275.
5. Friedrich Nietzsche, Die Geburt der Tragödie in
Werke, Vol. 1 (Munich: Carl Hanser, 1967), p. 77.
6. Lev Shestov, Na vesakh Iova (Paris: La sociéte
nouvelle d'Éditions Franco-Slaves, 1929), p. 42. All
further references to this work will be followed by the
letter "J" and page number.
7. Shestov, Umozrenie i otkrovenie (Paris: YMCA
Press, 1964), pp. 63-64.
8. F. M. Dostoevsky, Idiot in Sobranie sochinenii,
Vol. 6 (Moscow, 1958), p. 591.
9. Dostoevsky, Zapiski iz podpol'ya, SS, Vol. 4,
p. 142.
10. Dostoevsky, Besy, SS, Vol. 7, pp. 642-643.
11. Ibid., p. 640.
12. Shestov, Umozrenie, p. 192.

13. Dostoevsky, Besy, p. 124.

14. Soren Kierkegaard, The Concept of Dread, tr. Walter Lowrie (Princeton: Princeton University Press, 1944), p. 79.

15. Kierkegaard, Philosophical Fragments, tr. David F. Swenson (Princeton: Princeton University Press, 1936), p. 92.

16. Nikolai Berdyaev, The Russian Idea (New York: MacMillan, 1949), p. 259.

17. Kierkegaard, Concluding Unscientific Post-script, tr. David F. Swenson and Walter Lowrie (Princeton: Princeton University Press, 1941), p. 75.

18. V. V. Zenkovsky, A History of Russian Philosophy, Vol. 2, tr. George L. Kline (London: Routledge & Kegan Paul, 1953), p. 781.

19. Stephen Ross, Literature, pp. 56-57.

20. Harry Shaw, A Dictionary of Literary Terms (New York: McGraw-Hill, 1972), pp. 148-149.

21. Ibid., p. 149.

22. Sylvan Barnet, et al., A Dictionary of Literary, Dramatic, and Cinematic Terms, 2nd Ed. (Boston: Little, Brown & Co., 1971), p. 49.

23. Shestov, Kierkegaard and the Existential Philosophy, tr. Elinor Hewitt (Athens: Ohio University Press, 1969), p. 223.

## ESSAY IV

## THE MOVEMENT OF FAITH
## IN TOLSTOY'S CONFESSION

Tolstoy's Confession is the story of the spiritual crisis which its author experienced during the late 1870s, when the man who had written War and Peace and Anna Karenina came to believe that he had accomplished nothing in life, that his life was meaningless. Though there may be parallels between the torment of Levin in Anna Karenina and Tolstoy's own conflicts in the Confession, the latter piece was written in 1879, two years after the publication of the former, and represents a more developed reflection on the "problem of life."

Tolstoy's Confession may be viewed as a philosophical piece insofar as it is concerned with certain problems in metaphysics and epistemology: Tolstoy seeks a meaning in life which is not destroyed by death, and if this meaning can be known, he asks, then how may we come to know it? His approach to the difficulty, however, is not a philosophical one; the work lacks the analytical method, the argument from premise to conclusion, which ordinarily distinguishes philosophy. Tolstoy is not so much trying to advance a logical proposition in the Confession as to bring home his spiritual condition. Although he may confuse logical and psychological questions, this seems to contribute to the artistic and spiritual effect and to the sincerity of his endeavor.

It may be objected that for all its artistic and spiritual effect, the Confession is not in the strictest sense a part of the belles lettres: it is neither fiction, poetry nor drama. Nonetheless, Tolstoy does take an approach which is characteristic of literary expression. The Confession is a story, a tale of spiritual crisis, complete with plot, hero and a chronological resolution of the plot. It is a piece which has its origin in "emotion recollected in tranquility," to use Wordsworth's definition of poetry, where the main character, its author, is faced with a problem that is resolved in the end. Every stage of advancement has its corresponding metaphor in the Confession itself, and analogies may be found throughout Tolstoy's fiction. The Confession, then, represents a confluence of philosophy and literature, where the two disciplines merge into a single, passionate concern for faith.

The difficulty in readily classifying Tolstoy's Confession lies in its modern character, specifically in its existential character. Unlike other philosophical schools of thought—such as rationalism, empiricism or positivism—existentialism has established itself in the literary realm. As a part of existential philosophy and literature, the story of Tolstoy's spiritual turmoil addresses the problem of establishing a relationship between the world and the self other than one of alienation. For Tolstoy, the philosophical concern lends itself to a literary expression in which the redeemed self is born in a movement of faith that emerges as the fourth aspect of a four-dimensional change or metamorphosis within the individual. The four dimensions of the metamorphosis may be described as (1) the encounter with death, (2) the onset of despair, (3) the struggle for possibility and (4) the movement of faith. Let us see, then, how an analysis of the movement of faith in Tolstoy's Confession may be rendered in these terms.

## 1. The Encounter with Death

From the opening pages of the Confession it may be seen that the encounter with death is initiated by the Fall; like Adam, Tolstoy discovered that the Tree of Knowledge is not the Tree of Life. His Garden was the Orthodox Church in which he was christened, and the Fruit that tempted him came in the form of a rumor he heard one day at school to the effect that there is no God.[1] The serpent was right. We shall not surely die; if we eat we may become as the gods, not only knowing but devising the difference between good and evil.

Once Tolstoy consumes the Fruit, his eyes are open to contradiction, and he sees that the world is not good. Using the measuring stick of reason and ethics contained in the Fruit, he is quick to perceive that "people live just as everyone lives, yet they all live according to principles which not only have nothing in common with the teachings of doctrine but for the most part are opposed to them" (C, 95); he sees further that "the teachings of doctrine, which are accepted on trust and sustained by external pressure, gradually fade under the influence of knowledge and the experience of life, which are at odds with the teachings of doctrine" (C, 96).

The prohibition to eat the Fruit awakens a feeling of dread because it awakens a sense of freedom; a gasping "What if?" fills the emptiness of innocence, which in this case is the emptiness of the Orthodox teachings. Once he had acquired the knowledge of good and evil before which the doctrine gradually fades, Tolstoy came to maintain a belief in moral perfection which was soon transformed into "a belief in perfection in general, into a desire to be better not in the eyes of myself or God but in the eyes of other people," and this turned into a longing to be more powerful than others (C, 97). Here a connection between a sense of ethics and the operations of reason should be noted. First of all, attention is directed outward, toward the eyes and power of other people. Secondly, the focus on one's position in the world opens up a sense of balance: Tolstoy's ethical posture and worldly power are weighed against the morality and power of those around him. His desire to be better and more powerful than others reveals his concern for results, for a fixed state of being rather than a process of becoming. Such a concern is characteristic of reason and ethics, for both are oriented toward the "then" of an if-then way of existing: if I am to realize my desire to be better and more powerful than others, then I must behave in a manner prescribed by others. This is in fact the starting point for several characters in Tolstoy's fiction, including Levin in Anna Karenina, Ivan Il'ich, Father Sergius and Nekhlyudov in Resurrection.

As a fallen man, Tolstoy longs to become as the gods, and by replacing God with himself Tolstoy loses himself in his effort to be himself. Allowing himself to be determined by others, he arrives at the point where "there was not a crime I did not commit, and for all this my superiors praised me and considered me and still consider me a relatively moral man" (C, 98). From here it was only a short step to a position in which people became repugnant to him, and he became repugnant to himself; he understood that his belief in perfection was nothing more than a delusion. Although he could now see the lie of perfection, Tolstoy tells us, "I did not reject the rank bestowed upon me by these people—the rank of artist, poet and teacher" (C, 100).

Realizing that what he and his colleagues had thought to be reality was an illusion and that the self he had fostered was really no self, Tolstoy compares himself and the others to madmen who believe that all except themselves are mad (C, 101). He explains that in order to create self-importance for themselves, he and his fellow writers adopted the following line of thought:

> Everything that exists is rational.
> Further, everything that exists is
> evolving and is doing so through an
> enlightenment. The enlightenment in turn
> undergoes change through the distribution
> of books and periodicals. We are paid
> and respected for writing books and
> periodicals, and therefore we are the
> most useful and the best of people
> (C, 101).

Thus existence shaped by reason, ethics and natural necessity. This is the legacy of the Hegelian assertion
that the serpent was not a deceiver. The attraction lay
in the appeal to the natural light and an enlightenment
which offers the security of reason, ethics and natural
necessity, under the spell of which reality and illusion exchange places.

Aware only of the mirage of power, progress and
position, Tolstoy was conscious of neither life nor
death but only of the feeling that something was amiss:

> I was tormented, like any living indi-
> vidual, by questions of how to live bet-
> ter. I still did not understand that in
> answering that one must live for pro-
> gress, I was talking just like a person
> being carried in a boat along the waves
> and the wind, a person who replies with-
> out actually answering the primary and
> for him the only real question, 'Where
> are we to steer?' by saying, 'We are being
> carried somewhere' (C, 102).

The torment which begins to turn the individual about,
throwing him back upon himself, collides with the
herd's refusal to acknowledge that torment which is the
mark of individual existence apart from the herd. The
attempt to smother the agony of the loss of self by
pointing the individual toward progress or a rational
and necessary evolution only increases it, since this
amounts to an attempt to eliminate the individual self.
Thus the person is left in a limbo between himself and
the world, carried along by the system and unable to
steer himself back to himself.

It is the man adrift, the man who has labored himself into no self, the fallen man, who encounters the skull amid the wine cups and roses. For Tolstoy the encounter came in Paris on 25 March 1857, when François Riche was put to death for murder:

> Thus during my stay in Paris the spec-
> tacle of an execution revealed to me
> the feebleness of my superstitious belief
> in progress. When I saw how the head was
> severed from the body and heard the thud
> of each part as it fell into the box, I
> understood, not with my intellect but
> with my whole being, that no theories
> of the rationality of existence or of
> progress could justify this act (C, 102).

Another faculty has come into play: the whole being. It emerges opposite the feebleness and nothingness of a rationality that would deny the legitimacy of any such understanding. It is this displacement of the intellect that signals the reversal in direction from outwardness to inwardness.

Less than a week prior to the execution, on 19 March, Tolstoy wrote in his diary, "In the middle of the night I was suddenly tormented by an oncoming doubt about everything. . . . Why? What am I?"[2] And on 6 April he refers to the execution, saying, "He kissed the Gospel and then—death. What insanity!"[3] It is not enough that the crowd simply beheaded the man—it had to have his approval as well.

Here we must note the difference between the ef-fect of death on its witnesses and its effect on the person dying. One recalls, for example, that Pierre went through a similar experience when he saw an execu-tion by firing squad in War and Peace:

> From the moment Pierre had witnessed
> this terrible murder committed by people
> who did not want it, it was as if that
> spring which supported everything and
> presented itself as something living
> was suddenly torn from him, and all was
> thrown into a heap of meaningless gar-
> bage. Though he could not say why, faith
> was destroyed in him, faith in the bene-
> volence of the world, in humanity, in
> his own soul and in God. . . . He felt
> he did not have the power to return to

life and to faith.[4]

For the dying Andrey, on the other hand, death came as an awakening: "Yes, this was death," he says to himself. "I have died—I have awakened. Yes, death is an awakening!"[5] Although something has died in Pierre while something else has been born in Andrey, in both instances the transformation comes about in a disintegration of reason.

It is also important to note that the element of the _sudden_ creeps into consciousness in a manner that cannot be assimilated by the intellect. It has a sound, a thud, the finality of which puts an end to the rationality of the system; reality has been stuffed piecemeal into the box. Death turns out to be something completely different from what the individual expects it to be. He cannot formulate any thoughts about it, nor can he discover or devise any theories about it; rather, he is forced to move beyond the reality he has fashioned for himself.

The death of Tolstoy's brother Nikolai on 20 September 1860 added to the effect which the execution had produced in him, yet we find traces of this as early as 1852 in the shriek of horror at the odor coming from the coffin of the narrator's mother in Childhood:

> Only at that moment did I understand
> where that powerful, heavy odor was com-
> ing from, that odor which filled the
> room and mixed with the smell of the
> incense. And the thought that the face
> which a few days ago was filled with
> beauty and tenderness, the face I loved
> more than anything in the world, could
> arouse terror, revealed the bitter truth
> to me for the first time and filled my
> soul with despair.[6]

On the occasion of Nikolai's death Tolstoy wrote to A. A. Fet,

> Never in my life has anything ever made
> such an impression on me. He spoke the
> truth when he said there was nothing
> worse than death. . . . A few minutes
> before his death he dozed off and then
> suddenly regained consciousness and,
> filled with horror, he whispered, "What

can it be?' He saw the something that
was swallowing him into nothingness.[7]

Whereas death had previously been a mere nothing, a
dreamless sleep into which we fade after threescore and
ten years, it now presents itself as a something which
devours and swallows, a substance that negates all other possibility of substance. The time we spend in this
life now serves only to turn the object of love into
one of horror, and the nothingness perceived by Nikolai
inches no less toward Tolstoy himself. What had been a
complacent acquiesence of the intellect now becomes
the sobbing rebellion of the whole being.

The passing of Tolstoy's brother tore him away
from life, affecting him the same way that the death of
Nikolai in Anna Karenina affected Levin. As he lay
awake listening to the coughing of his dying brother,
the idea of death forcedly confronted Levin for the
first time:

> And this death which was here in his
> beloved brother, who was moaning half
> awake, out of habit calling indiscrim-
> inately now on God, now on the devil,
> was not as far away as it had once
> seemed. He felt it even within himself.
> If not today, then tomorrow; if not to-
> morrow, then in thirty years—wasn't it
> really all the same? And not only did
> he not know what this inevitable death
> was, not only had he never thought about
> it, but he did not know how nor did he
> dare to think about it. 'I am working, I
> want to do things, yet I had forgotten
> that all will end in—death.' He sat on
> his bed in the darkness, crouching and
> hugging his knees, holding his breath
> from the tension of thought. But the
> more he strained at the notion, the more
> clear it became to him that it was un-
> doubtedly so, that he had actually for-
> gotten, that he had overlooked in life
> one small detail, namely that death will
> come and all will end, that it wasn't
> even worth starting anything, and there
> was no way it could be helped. Yes, it
> was terrible, but it was so.[8]

This is the fear revealed in a handful of dust, and

death is as tangible as the dust itself—"he felt it within himself." It reduces not only the individual to dust but time and accomplishment as well; all possibility vanishes, eclipsed by the one certainty of death— "there was no way it could be helped." And there is no getting around this one little detail that divides the self against itself. The rational and necessary evolution which had been a source of reassurance has become something quite different.

We must note further that the encounter with death is not a physical one; it occurs rather on a metaphysical or spiritual level. Tolstoy in fact demonstrated his courage in the face of death time after time on the battlefield, and he was once very nearly killed by a bear while on a hunting trip. That the encounter does not necessarily pertain to any single event becomes more evident when nine years after the death of Nikolai it is repeated, this time in the absence of anyone dying. It was September, 1869, in what has since been referred to as the Arzamas agony. Tolstoy was on his way to Penza to buy an estate at a bargain price, when he put up for the night at an inn in Arzamas. And then it happened. "The horror came over him," as Henri Troyat describes it, "mixed with despair, 'as if he were about to vomit.' A geometric horror, 'a white and red horror, square,' the horror of the box."[9]

Tolstoy later worked this incident into a short story in 1884 called "Notes of a Madman." As the title of the work indicates, Tolstoy took this horror and depression, this spiritual nausea, to be a type of madness. In this case, however, the individual is left without the security of one who is irrevocably mad, whose madness is a refuge from the world; here it is existence itself that had gone mad. Further, Tolstoy is responsible for his madness to the extent that it is a symptom of his having failed to synthesize the eternal and temporal aspects of himself. Yet for the individual whose existence has been shaped by reason, ethics and natural necessity, in order to achieve the synthesis he must contract the madness, since the horror of the box ignites the passion which leads to the relationship between the self and itself and between the self and God. The sickness is itself the cure. It is this madness, this pathological state of horror and despair, that distinguishes the next dimension in the metamorphosis. Having tasted the horror of the box, Tolstoy will now drink the cup of despair to its bitter dregs.

## 2. The Onset of Despair

Tolstoy had contracted what Kierkegaard calls the sickness unto death. Indeed, it was in 1874, five years prior to the writing of the Confession, that Tolstoy claims despair set in. "I began to experience moments of confusion," he writes. "Life came to a stop, as if I didn't know how to live or what to do; I became lost and fell into despair" (C, 104). In despair the man is turned about and left entirely to himself; the coordinate system that had provided him with direction has been lost and with it the self it had shaped. But rather than meet the task of creating a self that can set out, like Abraham, without direction, the man in despair continues to clutch at the pieces of the crumbling structure, knowing all the while there is nothing to support the weight of his despair. Afraid to let go and afraid not to, he cannot move; he can only gape and stare and be afraid.

Despair in this case falls upon a man who enjoys health, the greatest possible success and lack of care, but this exaggerated well-being conspires to make death all the more unacceptable. Because despair is a condition of the lost spirit, it concerns the eternal aspect of the self; in the language of Jaspers, it permeates the encompassing that we are. And since it involves the eternal, the individual in despair is constantly falling into despair. The ability and the direction which might enable him to come out of it have been lost; this is the "coming to a stop," the impotence to act, the madness.

Having long since rejected a relationship with God, the encounter with death has led Tolstoy to an encounter with the nothingness which marks the absence of a God relationship. Yet in a sense the relationship is not actually absent because at this point its presence remains an impossibility. With the onset of despair the individual is thus abandoned to the geometric void of the box, lying atop the head and the body, so that instead of seeking a relation between the finite and the infinite, he lamely insists on the detachment of the finite from the devouring, decomposing nothingness that characterizes the finite.

Looking at Ivan Il'ich, we see that one of the horrors of despair is that the individual is cast into a state of forlornness from which there appears to be no escape: "He wept over his helplessness, over his terrible loneliness, over the cruelty of people, over the cruelty of God, over the absence of God."[10] The state of forlornness is a state of being locked inside the finite while being engulfed by the infinite, reduced to nothing not before God but before the heartless immensity of the surrounding spaces. In the awakening to forlornness the individual discovers for the first time that there is a vital part of himself which must remain forever hidden and isolated, incommensurably alone. In short, the individual discovers the self. He feels that if only he could give voice to the forlornness, then death might be less unbearable, less forlorn, for the horror lies in the prospect of dying alone and unable to give voice to the dying. The family and friends who cling to the system of propriety do not acknowledge Ivan Il'ich's dying because from the standpoint of the system there is nothing to acknowledge. Thus "Ivan Il'ich's main torment was the lie avowed for some reason by everyone, the lie that he was merely ill and not dying."[11]

The inner forlornness of the individual whose gaze is riveted to death finds the mirror image of death in his outward life as a small part of an infintie universe. Like Levin, he sees that "in infinite time, in infinite matter, in infinite space a bubble of an organism appears, and the bubble will last for a short time and then burst, and I am that bubble."[12] While the inward isolation had made death a horror, now the outward lack of isolation makes a horror of life. Here the self cannot distinguish itself from the universe or the world system; the body cannot be separated from the spatio-temporal continuum just as the spirit cannot enter into it. The finite and infinite aspects of the self thus remain divided and unrelated.

This is the milieu in which the seemingly childish and foolish questions of "Why?" and "What next?" arise; but, Tolstoy writes,

> . . . as soon as I have come up against them and have tried to resolve them, I am immediately convinced first of all that they are not childish and foolish questions, but the most vital and profound questions in life, and secondly that no matter how much I ponder them, there is no way I can resolve them (C, 105).

That the futile attempt to answer the foolish questions reveals their depth shows that neither the questions nor their resolution is as important as the passion in which they arise. Reason, which focuses solely on the stasis of outcome, deems them foolish and childish, so much stuff and nonsense. Just as Tolstoy encountered death not through his intellect but through his whole being, the profundity of the questions is not impressed upon the intellect, which looks to their content, but upon the whole being, which is the realm of the terror and the passion.

Tolstoy compares himself in his despair to a sick man who, like Ivan Il'ich, suddenly realizes that the ailment which "he had taken for a mere trifle is in fact the most important thing on earth, that it is death" (C, 105). The harder he tries to respond to the questions, the greater his consciousness of them, and therefore the deeper his despair; yet it seems there will be no end to the despair unless he can come up with an acceptable response. And as the despair increases, the ability to live decreases:

> It was as though I had lived a little,
> wandered a little, until I arrived at
> the precipice, and I clearly saw that
> there was nothing ahead except ruin.
> And there was no stopping, no turning
> back, no closing my eyes so I wouldn't
> see that there was nothing ahead except
> the deception of life and happiness and
> the reality of suffering and death, com-
> plete annihilation (C, 106).

The world is there, without us, and death becomes agonizing to the extent that we are aware of its indifference and the indifference of a material existence; and this is inseparable from a horror of life. In an essay titled On Life Tolstoy explains,

> If a man fears, he does not fear death,
> which he does not know, but life, which
> is the one thing he does know, both in
> his animal and rational existence. That
> feeling which is expressed in people as
> a fear of death is only a consciousness
> of the internal contradiction of life.[13]

The internal contradiction of life is that it is a spatio-temporal finitude standing opposite a spaceless and timeless infinity. Until a synthesis of the two is achieved, one can only cling to the ground of finitude and wait to be swallowed up by the nothingness of infinity. In order to be a something, in order to exist just once, the self must fade into nothingness; the one comes at the expense of the other. In despair the individual is caught between the two, unable to live or die.

Thus like Levin, Tolstoy was unable to make a move either within or without; the internal contradiction was pulling him in opposite directions. Thoughts of suicide came to him as a matter of course, even tempted him, so that he was afraid to remain in a room alone with a rope or to go hunting by himself. Think of it: the trembling hand gripping the coarseness of the rope, the eyes scanning the rafters along the ceiling, the gasping flight from the room to seek the company of the family only to dwell further on the rope and the room and the return to the room.

It is important to note that the temptation of suicide goes hand in hand with the hope of life; this is what makes the temptation a temptation and is the essence of the internal contradiction of life and of self. This is the self which in defiance Tolstoy is not willing to be, the self which in defiance he is tempted to destroy. In the act of suicide the will of the self is at its pinnacle, so that by doing away with itself the self attains the ultimate awareness of substance of will within and therefore achieves "authenticity." The individual thus places himself in the position of the power that determines his existence or nonexistence. In this sense suicide is a rebellion against God and against the trial of self-creation.

In order to better explain his anguish and despair Tolstoy relates an old fable about a traveler who clings to a branch in a well, with a wild beast above and a dragon below, both ready to devour him, while two mice gnaw at the branch. However, there are drops of honey on the leaves of the branch, and the traveler stretches out his tongue to lick them off. Says Tolstoy,

> Thus I cling to the branch of life,
> knowing that inevitably the dragon of
> death is waiting. . . . And I try to
> suck the honey which once consoled me,
> but this honey has lost its sweetness.
> . . . I see only the inescapable dragon
> and the mice, and I cannot turn my gaze

from them (C, 108).

Here we see that the encounter with death leads to an onset of despair in which one is hourly dying the death. Death is no longer the last thing, as Kierkegaard has pointed out, but is experienced continually in the internal collapse of time.[14] When death is not the last but continually the last it appears in the form of a truth for which all else is a lie and all other possibility closed. Such is the state of mind in which Levin "painfully felt that what he had referred to as his convictions was not only a lack of knowledge but it was a train of thought that made the knowledge he required impossible."[15] This in the Confession we read, "Now I cannot help seeing the days and nights rushing toward me and leading me to death. I see only this, and this alone is truth. All that remains is a lie" (C, 109). The task now is to reverse the truth and the lie, to open the way to the possibility that life may be the truth and death the lie. In order to be able to live and die, the question "without which life is impossible" must be answered: "Is there a meaning in my life which will not be inevitably destroyed by my coming death" (C, 111)? More than that, it must be answered in the affirmative when by all that is conceivable it can only be answered in the negative. The alternative is the lingering horror of the box and the temptation of the rope. The question arises in despair, and it is in despair that the struggle for possibility is initiated.

## 3. The Struggle for Possibility

The primary distinction between this dimension and the previous one is not that the despair has passed but that the individual now tries to move forward and bring together the finite and the infinite, the temporal and eternal. Here begins the struggle to determine whether or not the logically impossible may become "psychologically" possible. Tolstoy begins by rejecting the doctrine of progress which falsely taught that if he knew his place in the complexity of the evolving whole, then he would know himself (C, 112). If man and his world are in fact linked together in a system of evolution, the individual must direct his attention outside of himself in order to acquire a perspective of himself in relation to what he is. But this is precisely the source of Tolstoy's difficulty. Rather than examine the objective system, he must now establish a subjective individuality which may qualify the whole and encompass both the world and the personal perspective. If we think of life as what goes on in space and time, we must somehow move beyond the coordinates of space and time in order to arrive at a meaning in life. Tolstoy finds accordingly that the knowledge of one's place in the evolving whole is in inverse proportion to its applicability to the meaning of life (C, 113).

When he turns to science for an answer the results are the same for the same reason:

> The general relationship of the experimental sciences to the question of life may be expressed thusly: Question: Why do I live? Answer: In infinitely vast space, over an infinite duration of time, infinitely small particles undergo modifications of infinite complexity, and when you understand the laws of these modifications, then you will understand why you live (C, 113-114).

Science answers Tolstoy's question in terms of physics, chemistry and biology, when the inquiry concerns the spirit and not the laws that govern the functions and motions of the body. It seems that science can only respond to the question in a misunderstanding of it; what Tolstoy takes to be an inadequate answer is really no answer.

Looking elsewhere, Tolstoy turns to philosophy, whose task, as he sees it, is not so much to provide an answer as to put the question clearly. Here he discovers that to the question "What am I and what is the universe?" philosophy can merely reply, "All and nothing." And to the question "Why?" philosophy answers, "I do not know" (C, 116). Again, what Tolstoy takes to be an inadequate answer is really no answer; here science and philosophy can do no better than the silence of death itself.

In turning to science and philosophy for a solution Tolstoy is searching for something with which to measure himself; he is qualitatively that which is his measure. He realizes this as well as the fact that the person who decides the question of his own life decides another question—that of humanity as a whole (C, 115). This relationship is not to be confused with that between the individual and the evolving unit; viewed as a cog in the machine, the person is defined by the machine rather than by himself and has no substance apart from the machine. The question now before us, however, does not concern an objective humanity within the system but the subjective individual isolated from the system, so that the individual subjectively internalizes the race and then returns to the race. Insofar as a body of objective knowledge pertains to the external spatio-temporal process, turning to such knowledge amounts not only to turning away from the real question but extinguishes any relationship between the individual and humanity which might transcend the evolution of the unit in space and time. Tolstoy therefore introduces four of the wisest men—Socrates, Schopenhauer, Solomon and the Buddha—as single individuals who apart from a given network of objective knowledge have arrived at a personal and passionate expression of the problem facing Tolstoy.

Tolstoy focuses on the following line from Socrates: "We grow nearer to the truth to the extent that we grow farther from life. . . . The wise man seeks death all his life, and for this reason death is not terrifying to him" (C, 118).[16] Tolstoy understood this to mean that death is the only truth and life an illusion. Here one might object that Tolstoy has missed the point of Socrates' remark; when the Greek asserts that the wise man spends his life seeking and preparing for death, he is in fact giving meaning to life, and in no illusory fashion: we live inasmuch as we are engaged in dying the death. This, however, is not exactly the sort of meaning Tolstoy is after, even though he has indeed misunderstood Socrates. The Socratic search for knowledge, the daily discourse on virtue and the preparation for death all take place in a spatio-temporal progression in which the moment is simply a particle of time, not of eternity. Moreover, it is a truth for this life that Tolstoy seeks, not some revelation that can only come in death.

The difference between the knowledge Socrates offers and the meaning Tolstoy longs for is the difference between Socratic recollection and Kierkegaardian repetition. As Kierkegaard states it,

> The dialectic of repetition is easy,
> for what is repeated has been, other-
> wise it could not be repeated, but pre-
> cisely the fact that it has been gives
> to repetition the character of novelty.
> When the Greeks said that all knowledge
> is recollection they affirmed that all

that is has been; when one says that life
is a repetition one affirms that existence
which has been now becomes.[17]

So it is that Kierkegaard speaks of recollection as a
discarded garment and of repetition as an imperishable
one.[18] If repetition occurs in space and time, the possibility of repetition is a condition which at every
instant renews life in the world from outside that life
by renewing the life within from within. He does not
seek a knowledge that is fixed and unchanging in the
way Socratic knowledge is. In this sense Socratic knowledge is the knowledge acquired in the Fall, which has
it that man in ignorance is not in a state of innocence
but in a state of error if not sin. Consequently there
is no real difference between Socrates' striving for
virtue or his preparation for death and Tolstoy's earlier striving for moral perfection. Both succumb to the
serpent.

As a young man Tolstoy had read and respected
Schopenhauer; the influence of Schopenhauer on Tolstoy
can be seen, for example, in the concept of death in
War and Peace as an awakening. It may be recalled that
for Andrey overcoming the fear of death meant submit-
ting to death and resigning himself from life. The revelation that comes to the dying Andrey, however, is one
which may enable us to die but not to live. The Tolstoy
of the Confession can therefore no longer find solace
in Schopenhauer, who according to Tolstoy claims,

> The fact that we are so frightened of
> nonexistence, or that we long so to live,
> only signifies that we know nothing ex-
> cept this desire. Therefore, upon com-
> plete annihilation of the will all that
> remains for us, we who are fulfilled by
> that will, is of course nothingness;
> but on the other hand, for those in whom
> the will has been transformed and re-
> nounced, this world of ours which is so
> real, with all its suns and galaxies, is
> itself nothingness (C, 119).[19]

Like Tolstoy, Schopenhauer was unable to see beyond the
swallowing up of the finite by the infinite; the emptiness of existence, he says in Parerga und Paralipomena,
"finds its expression in the infinity of time and space
opposite the finitude of the individual in both."[20] It
is through an assertion of the will to live that Tol-

stoy renounces the will to live a life whose meaning is nullified by death, since life itself is then reduced to a mere nothing. As the world and the will that renounces itself degenerate into nothingness, the self likewise fades into nothingness; both the finite and the eternal are lost. Schopenhauer thus leaves Tolstoy where he started.

Tolstoy next turns to the Solomon of Ecclesiastes, a book which was not actually written by Solomon but rather dates from around the third century B.C. Quoting from Ecclesiastes, Tolstoy writes,

> All is vanity! . . . There is nothing
> new under the sun. . . . I have com-
> mitted my heart to knowing wisdom, mad-
> ness and folly; I discovered that even
> this was a languishing of the spirit.
> For in much wisdom there is much sorrow;
> and he who increases knowledge increases
> sorrow. . . . The wise die the same death
> as the foolish! And I came to despise
> life (C, 119-120).

These lines paraphrase what Tolstoy has already said: if not today, then tomorrow. Yet there is an important difference between Tolstoy's use of Ecclesiastes and the point of the book itself: "To sum up the whole matter: fear God, and keep the commandments, since this is the whole duty of man. For God will call all hidden deeds, good or bad, to judgement" (Ecclesiastes 12:13-14). Solomon's lamentation of life arises not in the absence of God as Tolstoy's does, but in the presence of a God whose ways we cannot fathom but who will call men to judgement in eternity, where all is revealed. Unlike Schopenhauer, Solomon does not completely negate life: it is better to be a living dog than a dead lion (Ecclesiastes 9:4). But Tolstoy fails to consider this and equates the two thinkers. Nonetheless, the author of Ecclesiastes is a man in despair; if the outcry is in the presence of God, it is in the absence of a relationship to God. One thing that Tolstoy and Solomon do have in common is the underlying feeling that they have been the victims of a bad joke, a cosmic prank. Solomon was granted the gift of wisdom only to find that all is vanity; Tolstoy was among the most gifted of men who call themselves writers, and he made the same unpleasant discovery.

Finally, Tolstoy relates the story of the young

Buddha, whose first sight of an old man, then a sick man, then a dead man led him to declare that life is evil (C, 121-122). But once again Tolstoy uses the tale for his own purposes. The Buddha does experience the encounter with death as indicated and even the ensuing despair, but he does not attach the negative moral epithet to life that Tolstoy does. He finds instead that life is suffering, which is neither good nor evil, and that one may overcome this suffering through a spiritual detachment from life; we must free ourselves from the bonds of existence. It should not be assumed, however, that Tolstoy knew very little about Buddhism; on the contrary, he had done a good deal of reading in Eastern religions. Yet he does seem to survey the ways of the Buddha through eyeglasses tinted with Schopenhauer.21 At any rate, the result of his examination of the four sages was only an increase in his despair: "There is no deceiving myself. All is vanity. Happy is he who was never born, death is better than life; we must rid ourselves of life" (C, 123).

Having given up on the knowledge of the wise men as a source of possibility, Tolstoy began to look at the people around him, the people of his own class, and in doing so he concluded that they could be placed into four categories (C, 123-125). First, there were those who lived in ignorance of the problem of life as presented by himself and the four savants. These were the ones who plod through life in a state of spiritual somnambulation, as though death would never come, for they have never experienced the encounter with death. Then there were the Epicureans, who flee the next day, engaging in an effort to destroy pain and time through the awful daring of a moment's surrender; they struggle in vain to gratify every sensual desire. As they plunge ever deeper into sensuality, they increase the depth of their despair and move farther and farther from themselves, sleeping through themselves as it were. The third category consisted of those few who had the power of reason and the strength of will to do away with an evil life. These were the nihilists who recognize that twice two is four and all else is trivial, and who have the courage to act on this; nothing is true, all things are permitted. Tolstoy deems this group the most worthy of respect, but he lacked the boldness required to be a part of it. Thus he places himself in the fourth group, those who see that life is evil but drag it out because they are too weak and too cowardly to become true nihilists. In devising these classifications, however, he cannot shake the feeling that he has gone wrong somewhere. At this point he begins to call reason into question, since reason is "the fruit of life, and yet it denies life" (C, 126). Reason cuts off the path to possibility. But Tolstoy is still in a state of confusion: reason is the fruit of the Tree of Knowledge, not that of the Tree of Life.

His next move, then, is to examine reason and try to clear up the confusion, and in doing so he finds that it was not in fact reason that had enabled him to continue to live:

> I wouldn't be speaking the truth if I were to say that it was through reason that I had arrived at this point without killing myself. Reason was at work, but it was working on a different level, something I cannot term other than a consciousness of life (C, 128).

Since reason had provided the basis for arranging the four categories mentioned above, Tolstoy felt compelled to turn to the millions whose lives are founded on something else. He explains,

> If I want to live and understand the meaning of life, then I must not search for this meaning among those who have lost it and want to destroy themselves. Rather, I must search among those millions of people who have lived and are still living, those who create life and take upon themselves the burden of their lives as well as our own (C, 129).

At this point Tolstoy draws a distinction between rational and irrational knowledge, declaring,

> Rational knowledge in the presence of the learned and the wise denies the meaning of life, but the vast masses of people, all of mankind, acknowledge meaning through an irrational knowledge. And this irrational knowledge is faith, the one thing which I could not accept. . . . According to faith, in order to understand the meaning of life, I must cast off reason, the very thing for which meaning was necessary (C, 130).

117

Reason had raised the question, but in order to answer it, reason must be abandoned. But is this really the case? Does the question not instead arise in an emotion, in a movement of the spirit, at which point the intellect tries to formulate a response? Tolstoy himself indicated that he experienced the encounter with death not through the intellect but with his whole being. And it is not that the intellect cannot respond, but that it cannot respond in a manner acceptable to the spirit, which seeks not by means of rationality but with lamentation.

Regarding the relation between the finite and the infinite, Tolstoy found that reason can only equate the finite with the finite and the infinite with the infinite, so that there can be no relation between them:

> I understood that I could not search
> for an answer to my question in ra-
> tional knowledge. The answer provided
> by rational knowledge is merely an in-
> dication that an answer can only be had
> by formulating the question of life in
> a different way, that is, only when the
> question of the relation between the
> finite and the infinite is brought into
> consideration (C, 131-132).

Here it may be seen that in the struggle for possibility Tolstoy is probing the limits of reason in an effort to apprehand the Other to reason, which is absolutely different because it lies outside the scope of the intellectual equipment we use to shape existence and experience. As Kierkegaard states it, since the Other to reason is absolutely different, "there is no mark by which it could be distinguished. When qualified as absolutely different it seems on the verge of disclosure, but this is not the case; for Reason cannot even conceive of an absolute unlikeness."22 By pushing reason to its limits Tolstoy came to understand that "no matter how irrational and unattractive the answers given by faith, they have the advantage of bringing to every reply a relation of the finite to the infinite, without which there can be no reply" (C, 132).

Insofar as it involves a relationship of the finite to the infinite, faith rests on a paradox that emerges at the limits of reason. In faith the eternal condition of the self is given in time, in a life lived in time, so that the temporal is gained through the eternal, which is to acquire the possibility of living. Because this union occurs at the limits of reason, the faith which rests on the paradox is the issue of an association between reason and the paradox: it is reason trying to comprehend the condition that makes it paradoxical. So it is that the answers given by faith are so unattractive, even offensive to reason. If the paradox, then, opens the door to possibility, it is possibility resting on the absurd. Thus considered, faith is the passion by virtue of which life from the eternal point of view is rendered possible in the temporal and finite world. This is why we hear Tolstoy saying, "Faith is the knowledge of the meaning of life whereby the individual does not destroy himself but lives. Faith is the force of life" (C, 133).

In order to avoid unnecessary confusion, it should be noted that Tolstoy uses the word "knowledge" in a rather peculiar sense; in place of "the knowledge of the meaning of life" and "the force of life" he could just as well have substituted Kierkegaard's "passion." As a passionate condition of the spirit, the force of life or faith is the opposite of despair, or in the language of Tolstoy, the knowledge of the meaning of life is the opposite of despair. Thus he writes,

> I came to understand that the most profound wisdom of mankind is harbored in the answers given by faith, and I did not have the right to deny them on grounds of reason, and that above all, these answers alone can respond to the question of life (C, 135).

In order to better comprehend the nature of faith, Tolstoy began to question those people of his own class who claimed to be believers, but he discovered no more than a counterfeit faith, one which only "clouded the meaning of life" (C, 135). He was not looking for arguments or demonstrations resting on reason but for actions or manifestations of the force of life that come in spite of reason. This does not mean that he wanted to find a basis for ethical behavior but rather for the possibility of faith. Ethics or morality pertains to the actions themselves, apart from a God relationship or a relationship to the eternal upon which actions in the temporal are grounded; this is the relationship Tolstoy requires, and this ethics cannot provide.

When he turned to the believers among the simple

and the poor Tolstoy found that here too there were
"superstitions" mixed with the truths of Christianity,
but with a difference: the superstitions of the believers in his own class were unnecessary to them,
while among those of the laboring class the superstitions formed an integral part of their lives—they were
as they believed:

> I began to focus on the life and the
> religious beliefs of the people, and
> the closer I looked, the more I was
> convinced that they possessed a genuine
> faith, that their faith was indispensable
> to them; it alone gives them meaning and
> the possibility of life (C, 137).

Here life was the truth and death the lie. This was ev-
idenced by the fact that "in contrast to the peaceful
death, a death without terror and despair, which is the
rarest exception in our class, it is the tormenting,
unyielding and sorrowful death that is the exception
among the people" (C, 138). Tolstoy's image of the
"poor and simple folk" was no doubt an idyllic one, but
this is beside the point. What is important is that he
measures the ability to give meaning to life according
to the attitude toward death; death is for all, but
each has his own death. Further, this distinction may
be applied not only to the dying but to the witnesses
of death as well. Consider, for example, the following
passage from Anna Karenina:

> Levin did not consider himself wise,
> but he could not help knowing that he
> was more intelligent than his wife and
> Agaf'ya Mikhailovna, and he could not
> help knowing that when he thought of
> death with all the might of his soul,
> he still could not fathom it. He also
> knew that many wiser men, whose thoughts
> on death he had read, had pondered it
> and did not know one hundredth of what
> his wife and Agaf'ya Mikhailovna knew.
> Whatever differences there may have been
> between these two women, . . . they were
> completely alike in this. Both un-
> doubtedly knew what life and death were,
> and although there was no way they could
> answer or even understand the questions
> that presented themselves to Levin,
> neither of them doubted the significance

> of the phenomenon and were entirely of
> the same disposition, not only between
> themselves but in sharing this view with
> millions of people who had looked upon
> death. The proof that they firmly knew
> what death was lay in the fact that they
> knew without a second's hesitation what
> had to be done with the dying and did
> not fear them. Levin, however, and others
> like him, although they could say a great
> deal about death, obviously did not know
> because they feared death and had no idea
> of what must be done when people are dy-
> ing. If Levin were now alone with his
> brother Nikolai, he would look upon him
> with horror and would wait with a still
> greater horror and would know of nothing
> else to do.[23]

For the man in despair, death is the nothingness
that engulfs, the infinity that swallows up the finite.
For the man of faith, seeing oneself as part of the infinite is not a source of despair but rather means seeing oneself outside of space and time, in the context
of a God relationship. By grounding his temporal life
in the eternal, he grounds himself in the absolute Thou
as the power that posits him, and it is the historical
death, not the self, that is swallowed up. So it is
that in the former case death appears to be the sole
reality, while in the latter it is an illusion. Tolstoy
concluded therefore that human life in general is not
evil and meaningless but his life in particular, the
life of the author of War and Peace and Anna Karenina.
In order for life to have the possibility of meaning,
Tolstoy saw that he must create possibility in his own
life, and this meant that his life must be devoted to
life and passionately so, rather than to himself.

Alternating between joy over a loving God who creates the possibility of life and the despair that makes
life impossible, Tolstoy found that he could live only
when he believed, when he rested everything on the absurd: "To know God and to live come to one and the same
thing—God is life" (C, 144). It is significant that
Tolstoy takes this new understanding of life to be a
return to the religious spirit of his childhood; here
we see a repetition of life, a coming to be by virtue
of a higher will for whom all things are possible. And
in Tolstoy's case, as in Job's, the repetition came
about when "all conceivable human certitude and proba-

121

bility pronounced it impossible."[24] To declare that God is life is to declare that life is a repetition of life, every instant and within the single instant renewed by God, and not part of a system that builds on itself and in which the individual must find his proper slot. The torment of the struggle for possibility therefore comes of a "wrestling match in which the universal breaks with the exception, breaks with it in strife, and strengthens it by this conflict."[25] In the struggle with the universal there is also a struggle with the eternal in which the eternal aspect of the self finds its strength; thus Jacob did battle with the angel.

Once he had perceived the folly of reason and the truth of faith, Tolstoy tells us that it was as if he had found himself alone in a boat going downstream with other boats, whose navigators assured him that there could be no other direction. Suddenly he realized that he would be destroyed in the rapids ahead, and with all his strength he began rowing upstream, back to the shore. "The shore was God," he explains, "the stream was tradition, and the oars were the free will given to me to make it to shore" (C, 145). Tradition in this case is tradition molded by reason, ethics and natural necessity; it is the tradition which Tolstoy and his colleagues had adopted in their doctrine of enlightenment. Thus when he compared the members of his own class to the working people he concluded that

> . . . God created man in such a way that
> every man can either save his own soul
> or destroy it. Man's task in life is to
> save his soul. In order to save his soul
> he must live according to the ways of God,
> and in order to live according to the
> ways of God he must renounce the sensual
> pleasures of life; one must labor, suffer
> and be kind and humble (C, 146).

Although Tolstoy appears to be on the verge of moralizing here, the thing we must note is the idea that the way to God is open to all because every person is capable of passion; where there is human life there is the possibility of faith.

However, Tolstoy, like Levin, continued to feel ill at ease with the Church ritual which was so important to the people; it seemed to him that the patterns of gesture and recitation incorporated in the religious institution were designed to prevent religious experience. Elaborating on this point, Carl Jung tells us,

> What is usually and generally called
> 'religion' is to such an amazing degree
> a substitute that I ask myself seriously
> whether this kind of 'religion,' which I
> prefer to call a creed, has not an im-
> portant function in human society. The
> substitution has the obvious purpose of
> replacing immediate experience by a choice
> of suitable symbols invested in a solidly
> organized dogma or ritual. The Catholic
> church maintains them by her indisputable
> authority, the Protestant church (if this
> term is still applicable) by insistence
> on faith and the evangelical message. As
> long as these two principles work, people
> are effectively defended and shielded
> against immediate religious experience.26

Rather than acknowledge the Church as something which
protects man from the God relationship, Tolstoy rein-
terpreted the significance of the Church, claiming that
it formed a basis for the union of all men in love, so
that through love men may be brought to the truth (C,
148-149). Whatever we may say about this view of the
Church, it is important to note that it is indeed love
for his fellow as determined by his love for God that
secures for man the possibility of authentic selfhood,
which is the possibility of creating a God relationship.
This love cannot be discovered by reason, and again
like Levin, Tolstoy realized that

> . . . reason discovered the struggle for
> existence and the law demanding the suf-
> focation of all who hinder the satisfac-
> tion of my desires. This is the conclu-
> sion of reason. But to love one's fellow
> man reason could not discover because
> this is not reasonable.27

Nor could doctrine reveal the love for one's fellow man. The passion which is unspeakable is lost in
the language of the doctrine; the truth and the spirit
of the Law are lost to the stone it is carved on, until
"the religious teaching itself destroys the very thing
it set out to produce" (C, 153). Jaspers has noted in
this connection that

> . . . the unfulfillment of communication

and the severity of its miscarriage become the revelation of a depth which nothing but transcendence can fill. . . .
Detached from this as permanent truth,
instead of being itself, truth degenerates into a knowledge of something,
to a finished satisfaction, instead of
a consuming demand in temporal existence.[28]

Like the sculptor who tried to capture a god in stone,
the doctrine tries to take hold of the passion in traps
that are not of its essence. In passing itself off as a
statement of eternal truth, the doctrine falls prey to
a contented complacency, and the Church becomes more
concerned with the external affairs of the world and
with the world's acceptance of doctrine than with the
internal life of the single individual. This is why the
Church has been so harsh with heretics; it has deemed
that there is no worse enemy than a child gone astray.
So it is that the Gospel was held up to the lips of the
condemned François Riche before they lopped off his
head.

This tie with human—or inhuman—affairs, with
wars and executions, disturbed Tolstoy more than anything else in his attempts to understand the role of
the Church and the doctrine it insisted upon (C, 153),
and this is why he decided that with the truth of the
people's beliefs there was also error (C, 156). The
error is that which Father Sergius discovered in himself after his visit with Pashenka: he realized that
through the glorification of the doctrine he had been
living for the sake of man, for his own sake, while using God as a pretext.[29] Thus we see that in order for
life to have a possibility of meaning, it is necessary
to penetrate the limit where the incomprehensible begins, and to do this something other than rational
knowledge or Church doctrine is required. Having
glimpsed that possibility which can be voiced only in
the form of paradox and contradiction, Tolstoy must
now complete the metamorphosis through the movement of
faith which rests on paradox, on the Other to reason.

## 4. The Movement of Faith

The movement of faith arises as the fourth aspect
of the change in the individual when the struggle for
possibility reaches the absurd as the sole support for
possibility. Here the absurd is what Tolstoy calls the
"inevitably incomprehensible" ("neizbezhno neob"yasni-

moe") when he says,

> I shall not seek an explanation of all
> things. I know that the explanation of
> all things, like the origin of all things,
> must remain hidden in infinity. But I do
> want to understand, so that I might be
> brought to the inevitably incomprehensi-
> ble; I want all that is incomprehensible
> to be such not because the demands of
> reason and the intellect are not sound
> (they are sound and apart from them I
> understand nothing), but because I per-
> ceive the limits of the intellect. I
> want to understand, so that any instance
> of the incomprehensible occurs as a ne-
> cessity of reason, and not as an obliga-
> tion to believe (C, 156-157).

The absurd arises as a "necessity of reason" in that it
is reason's Other, shaped by the limiting outlines of
reason. The absurd is not something we are obliged to
believe but is the abyss into which we must leap from
the springboard of the intellect and above which we
must dwell despite the temptations of the intellect.
The Other to reason is the absolute Other to existence
molded by reason, and the relationship to the absolute
Other which is achieved in the movement of faith is absolute; that is, it is a completely self-determined relationship, and there is nothing from which it may be
derived. Because rationality acknowledges no Other, the
relationship must be effected by the single individual
in isolation from the universal realm of rationality.
And because it lies within the single individual, the
absolute relationship to the absolute Other is a personal relationship to the absolute Thou, to a personal
God.

At this juncture the language of analysis dwindles,
and Tolstoy comes to describe the movement of faith in
terms of a dream. In the dream he is suspended between
an infinite depth which horrifies him and an infinite
height which reassures him. He tells us,

> As it happens in a dream, the mechanism
> by which I am supported seems quite nat-
> ural, understandable and beyond doubt,
> in spite of the fact that when I am awake
> the mechanism is completely incomprehen-
> sible. In my sleep I am even astonished

that I had not understood this before;
it seems that there is a pillar beside
me, and there is no doubt of the solidity
of the pillar, even though it has nothing
to stand on. A cord is somehow very clev-
erly yet very simply attached to the pillar, leading out from it, and if you
place the middle of your body on the cord
and look up, there cannot even be a question of falling (C, 159).

We discover that as the allegorical images employed in the work ascend from the well to the stream
to the aerial suspension, there is a corresponding ascent in the consciousness of self, moving from an un-
awareness of having an eternal self to the possibility
of having a self that lives in a relation between the
finite and the infinite directly before God. The upshot
of it all is that reason, which had demanded a meaning
in life without which life is impossible, is lost in
the leap by which Tolstoy is now suspended in a dream,
so that the possibility of life is regained by virtue
of the incomprehensible. In the words of Kierkegaard,
"the movement of faith must always be performed by virtue of the absurd, and—this is very important—in such
a way that the things of the world are not lost but
eternally regained."30

Again, the four aspects of the change in the individual—the encounter with death, the onset of despair, the struggle for possibility and the movement of
faith—are dimensional rather than evolutionary; one
aspect does not progress into another to be left behind
but rather each aspect emanates from and returns to the
others. Because the movement of faith which consummates
the metamorphosis is dimensional, it falls back on itself in a repetition of itself, and this is what makes
the movement a becoming, a rebirth. Moreover, since the
act of the will arises from an underlying condition,
that is, from a structure of the if-then, and since
reason, ethics and natural necessity are set aside in
making the movement of faith, the movement itself is
not an act of will in that it is not motivated by a
desire for salvation or any other desire, for this
would make it reasonable. Indeed, it is born of itself
when the individual is reborn in the God relationship,
and yet it is the issue of that relationship. Tolstoy
therefore finds himself suspended in the midst of the
abyss above and below, and this is what makes faith a
miracle, a gift of God.

126

In Tolstoy's fiction, as well as in his life, we see a repetition of the movement. In <u>War and Peace</u>, for example, Pierre finally arrives at the point where the

> . . . terrible question 'Why?' which had previously destroyed all his intellectual constructions now no longer existed for him. To the question 'Why?' there was now a simple answer fixed in his soul: because God <u>is</u>, that God without whose will not a single hair falls from a man's head.[31]

In <u>Anna Karenina</u> Levin rediscovers the answer to the question of life in the force and passion of life. The peasant Fëdor, for example, reminds him of that simple answer which Pierre had come to: we live for God. Here Levin ruminates,

> To live not for oneself but for God. For what God? And what could be more meaningless than what Fëdor had said? He said that we mustn't live for ourselves or for the things we understand, the things which attract us and which we desire, but we must live for something beyond comprehension, for God, whom no one can either understand or define. So? Did I fail to understand Fëdor's meaningless words? And having understood them, did I doubt the justice of them? Did I find them stupid, vague, inaccurate? No, I did understand them, precisely as he understands them, I understood completely and more clearly than I understand anything in life, and never in my life have I doubted, nor am I able to doubt.[32]

That which is most sublime, like that which is most terrible, is not to be seen or heard or read about but to be lived. Both in his works and in his life Tolstoy oscillated from despair to faith and back again, and, as it happens with most of us, he was never farther from the truth than when he thought he had found it. This too is why the movement must be repeated in a dimensional metamorphosis rather than an evolutionary one. To quote once more from Jaspers, "I believe only by doubting that I believe."[33]

It may be seen that a belief in an infinite Being outside of space, time and causality, a God for whom all things are possible, is implicit in Tolstoy's doubt, in his question about the meaning of life. Unlike a character in a novel who in the end is no longer troubled by the aim of life, Tolstoy continued in his efforts to clarify that aim after he had been converted, if indeed one may speak of conversion in this connection at all. It seems rather dubious to identify the movement of faith with conversion, since a conversion that must repeat itself may be construed as no conversion. The critics in fact are not in agreement as to what Tolstoy's "conversion" was like, although the term is widely used in reference to Tolstoy. According to Aylmer Maude, for example,

> . . . what is unusual about the story of Tolstoy's conversion is that it came so late in life and so gradually, and that the intellect played so large a part in it. Some men take religion at the prompting of the heart, others at the prompting of the brain; and Tolstoy belongs to the latter category, not from lack of heart, but strong as are his emotions, his intellectual power is stronger still.[34]

Fueloep-Miller, on the other hand, does not by any means take Tolstoy's "conversion" to be a gradual one. "For Tolstoy," he says, "his conversion was not so much the turning point; it was rather the breaking point."[35]

The confusion surrounding the nature of Tolstoy's so-called conversion suggests that the movement of faith cannot be equated with conversion. Jaspers, for example, has spoken of Nietzsche's leap, but what would it be like to say that Nietzsche was converted? For conversion means Seeing the Light, Finding the Way or the One Path to Truth, and, as we have seen, truth found degenerates into a settled complacency, into no truth. Of course it may be asked whether or not Tolstoy ever actually made the movement of faith, but such a question is not quite to the point. The vital thing is that the concept of a movement of faith by virtue of the absurd is to be found in the Confession. If one must answer this question, it may be that Tolstoy did not make the movement until that night in 1910 shortly before his death, when he set out, like Abraham, knowing not where he was to go. Here we see that the sig-

nificance of spiritual crisis is that it generates crisis; faith is lived and decisively worked for in fear
and trembling, but it is never lived through. This is
what makes faith so terrible and at the same time so
wonderful; if it comes in terror, it is crowned with
indescribable joy.

Has Tolstoy, then, either answered or eliminated
the question of life? The opinions in this regard, like
most opinions on Tolstoy, are varied. Turgenev, for instance, could find in the Confession only a negation of
life. In a letter to D. V. Grigorovich he writes,

> A few days ago I received from a very
> nice Moscow lady L. Tolstoy's Confes-
> sion, which the censor has forbidden.
> I read it with great interest; it is
> quite remarkable in its sincerity,
> honesty and power of expression. But
> it all rests on misleading premises,
> and in the end it leads to the darkest
> denial of any human life.[36]

According to E. B. Greenwood, however, "Tolstoy's whole
endeavor in A Confession is to try to show that he and
those like him are mistaken in supposing that there is
'some evil irony in the fact that we suffer and die.'"[37]
In either case the question has been answered; in the
negative on Turgenev's view, in the affirmative on
Greenwood's. Yet in the light of what has been dis-
cussed, both interpretations are wrongheaded. Again,
truth found is no truth, and an answer formulated to
the question of life, be it yes or no, reflects a misunderstanding of the question. Here we see the significance of Levin's discovery that thought could not answer his question: "It is incommensurable with the question; the answer came from life itself."[38] The life
which reveals itself in the seeking is more vital than
the finding, and the asking of the question is more vital than the answering of it: the lamentation weighs
heavier than the understanding, heavier than the sand
of the sea. Thus the eyes close, we are left to our
closet, and the lamentation, like a prayer, seeks its
voice.

## NOTES

1. L. N. Tolstoy, Ispoved' in Sobranie sochinenii,
Vol. 16 (Moscow, 1964), p. 94. All further reference to
this work will be followed by the letter "C" and page

number.

2. Tolstoy, <u>Dnevniki</u>, <u>SS</u>, Vol. 19, p. 191.
3. Ibid.
4. Tolstoy, <u>Voina i mir</u>, <u>SS</u>, Vol. 7, p. 53.
5. Ibid., p. 95.
6. Tolstoy, <u>Detstvo</u>, <u>SS</u>, Vol. 1, p. 113.
7. Tolstoy, <u>Pis'ma</u>, <u>SS</u>, Vol. 17, p. 219.
8. Tolstoy, <u>Anna Karenina</u>, <u>SS</u>, Vol. 8, pp. 408-409.
9. Henri Troyat, <u>Tolstoi</u> (Paris: Fayard, 1965), p. 390.
10. Tolstoy, <u>Smert' Ivana Il'icha</u>, <u>SS</u>, Vol. 12, p. 106.
11. Ibid., p. 98.
12. Tolstoy, Anna Karenina, Vol. 9, p. 412.
13. Tolstoy, <u>O zhizni</u> in <u>Polnoe sobranie sochinenii</u>, Vol. 26 (Moscow, 1957), p. 400.
14. Soren Kierkegaard, <u>The Sickness unto Death</u>, tr. Walter Lowrie (Princeton: Princeton University Press, 1946), p. 25.
15. Tolstoy, <u>Anna Karenina</u>, Vol. 9, p. 409.
16. See Plato, <u>Phaedo</u>, tr. Hugh Tredennick in <u>The Collected Dialogues</u>, ed. Edith Hamilton and Huntington Cairns (Princeton: Princeton University Press, 1969), pp. 44-52.
17. Kierkegaard, <u>Repetition</u>, tr. Walter Lowrie (Princeton: Princeton University Press, 1941), p. 34.
18. Ibid., p. 4.
19. See Arthur Schopenhauer, <u>Parerga und Paralipomena</u> in <u>Werke</u>, Vol. 5 (Leipzig: Inselverlag, 1922), p. 423.
20. Ibid., p. 307.
21. "Brahmanism and Buddhism," says Schopenhauer, "have a basic character of <u>idealism</u> and <u>pessimism</u>, since they understand the world as a dream-like existence and consider life as the result of our guilt" (<u>Parerga</u>, p. 412).
22. Kierkegaard, <u>Philosophical Fragments</u>, tr. David F. Swenson (Princeton: Princeton University Press, 1936), p. 35.
23. Tolstoy, <u>Anna Karenina</u>, Vol. 9, pp. 75-76.
24. Kierkegaard, <u>Repetition</u>, p. 133.
25. Ibid., p. 152.
26. Carl Jung, <u>Psychology and Religion</u> (New Haven: Yale University Press, 1938), pp. 52-53.
27. Tolstoy, <u>Anna Karenina</u>, Vol. 9, p. 422.
28. Karl Jaspers, <u>Vernunft und Existenz</u> (Bremen: Johs. Storm, 1949), p. 80.
29. Tolstoy, <u>Otets Sergii</u>, <u>SS</u>, Vol. 12, p. 409.
30. Kierkegaard, <u>Fear and Trembling</u>, tr. Robert Payne (London: Oxford University Press, 1939), p. 47.

31. Tolstoy, Voina, Vol. 7, pp. 234-235.
32. Tolstoy, Anna Karenina, Vol. 9, pp. 419-420.
33. Jaspers, Vernunft, p. 93.
34. Aylmer Maude, The Life of Tolstoy, Vol. 1, 5th Ed. (New York: Dodd, Mead and Co., 1911), p. 400.
35. Rene Fueloep-Miller, "Tolstoy the Apostolic Crusader," Russian Review, 19 (1960), 106.
36. I. S. Turgenev, Pis'ma in Polnoe sobranie sochinenii, Vol. 28 (Leningrad, 1968), p. 89.
37. E. B. Greenwood, Tolstoy: The Comprehensive Vision (New York: St. Martin's Press, 1975), p. 120.
38. Tolstoy, Anna Karenina, Vol. 9, p. 422.

# ESSAY V

## PHYSICS, PHILOSOPHY AND MYSTICISM

Philosophy's attempts to deal with faith have led to certain transformations of thought which have been significant to other disciplines. With the developments that have come about in physics over the past decades, philosophy has become more and more essential to the thinking of physicists. Just as philosophy has seen a shift away from speculative thought, so too has physics experienced a shift away from the cause-and-effect way of thinking about the world. Many physicists have thus had occasion to examine the metaphysics of physics as it were and have found that the new physics has certain affinities with philosophical and religious currents of thought.

Robert Oppenheimer, Niels Bohr and Werner Heisenberg are among the physicists who have noted parallels between modern physics and Eastern mysticism,[1] but until the publication of Fritjof Capra's Tao of Physics in 1975, no single physicist had examined the similarities at length. Although Capra's piece met with a good deal of popularity, it did not go uncriticized. In a brief but penetrating review of the book Dean R. Fowler acknowledges Capra's demonstration of the "numerous points of contact between the physics of the West and the mysticism of the East," yet he registers the following complaint:

> The frustration I find in Capra's work is his failure to explore in any depth the underlying reason why there is a striking similarity between the physicist's description of the microcosm and the mystic's description of the macrocosm. Capra's answer, which may be gleaned from the pages of his book, is rooted in a philosophical idealism. Science and mysticism are not unified as disciplines. Instead the unification is a function of the mind in its rational and intuitive dimensions.[2]

In this essay I shall offer a reply in behalf of Capra and others who have noted congruities between physics and mysticism but who, like Capra, have failed to establish any real philosophical groundwork for their observations. As I shall argue, the metaphysics of subjectivity generated by existential philosophy reinforces the parallels pointed out by Capra. Here the philosopher's expression of self-to-self and self-to-world relationships may provide the missing link which has frustrated critics such as Fowler.

1

In order to develop a clear picture of the parallels between modern physics and Eastern mysticism, we should do well to begin by elucidating a few points on quantum theory. The most basic aspect of quantum physics is the wave/particle vision of subatomic entities. Physicists have found, in other words, that such entities sometimes exhibit the properties of particles, sometimes of waves, depending on the method and circumstances of observation. In regard to the nucleus of an atom, for example, Eddington cautions us about thinking of it as "a sort of billiard ball," explaining that it is more accurately envisioned as a "system of waves."[3]

When we use the term "wave," however, we must be careful not to think of ordinary waves such as sound waves or those made by a pebble tossed into a pond. Despite the mental cramp of it all, we are faced with trying to imagine what physicists refer to as "probability waves" or "tendencies to exist." That is, the wave characteristics of subatomic particles reflect a peculiar situation in which a given entity never exists in a definite place but only shows a tendency to be there.[4] In this connection Oppenheimer writes,

> To what appeared to be the simplest questions, we will tend to give either no answer or an answer which will at first sight be reminiscent more of a strange catechism than of the straightforward affirmatives of physical science. If we ask, for instance, whether the position of the electron remains the same, we must say 'no'; if we ask whether the electron's position changes with time, we must say 'no'; if we ask whether the electron is at rest, we must say 'no'; if we ask whether it is in motion, we must say 'no.'[5]

Another way of describing this Alice-in-Wonderland picture is to say that like waves, subatomic particles have no meaning as isolated entities or as fixed, static objects. The particles exist, rather, as dynamic correlations or interconnections, as processes. In the words of Bohr, "isolated material particles are abstractions, their properties on the quantum theory being definable only through their interaction with other systems."[6] An abstraction of the particle is derived, for instance, from an interaction between an observed system and an observing system structured around a particle accelerator at position A and a particle target at position B. Here the particle is defined as that event which occurs from the time it leaves A to the time it has interacted at B. Further, the time interval itself frames "the finite magnitude of the quantum of action," which, as Bohr explains, "prevents altogether a sharp distinction being made between a phenomenon and the agency by which it is observed."[7] To this it may be helpful to add an insight from Capra: "The particle constitutes an intermediate system connecting the processes at A and B. It exists and has meaning only in this context."[8] At this juncture an important parallel between modern physics and Eastern mysticism arises. Consider, for example, the following words of Krishna from the Bhagavad Gita: "Whatever being is born, immovable or moving, know . . . that it (arises) from the union of the field and the knower of the field."[9]

Viewing the subatomic entity as a relation or process and not as an object filling the void is conceptually rooted in the space/time, matter/energy continuum posited by relativistic physics. Field theory models of the microscopic and macroscopic universe have their foundation in this underlying unity. Einstein demonstrated, for example, that matter determines the curvature of space, while the curvature of space determines the motion of matter. The gravitational field is precisely the curvature of space/time, and where there is no matter or energy, there is no space or time. Quoting Einstein, Capra adds, "We may therefore regard matter as being constituted by the regions of space in which the field is extremely intense."[10] On the microscopic scale, the quantum particle is the region of high field concentration in the probability wave, and if we must speak of a void, it is the area of low field concentration, of a low tendency to exist. Here Capra tells us, "Like the Eastern Void, the 'physical vacuum' . . . is not a state of mere nothingness, but contains the potentiality for all forms of the particle world."[11] The Eastern Void which Capra compares to the physical vacuum turns up in the Upanishads, for example, as "the Unmanifest" from which all things, physical and spiritual, arise.[12]

   If an underlying void or nothingness lies behind
all forms of the particle world, it likewise structures
the forms of being in general. Compare this notion to
the Self of which Krishna speaks in the Gita: "And
(yet) beings do not rest in Me: behold my divine mystery (yoga). My Self, which is the source of beings,
sustains all beings but does not rest in them."[13] From
the point of view of modern physics as well as Eastern
mysticism, then, all events, all beings, are intercon-
nected through their relation to the underlying and
unifying void or continuum (Krishna's Self) and not by
virtue of a chain of cause and effect. "We saw in the
very heart of the physical world," says Oppenheimer,
"an end of that complete causality which had seemed so
inherent a feature of Newtonian physics."[14] There is no
banging together of the many, just a boiling up of the
one.

   The loss of causality is more shaking than it may
seem at first glance. Oppenheimer goes on to say that
the early period of discovery in this century was "a
time of creation; there was terror as well as exalta-
tion in their eyes."[15] For the physicist whose entire
vision of reality—and of himself—rests on causality,
the loss of causality is akin to Abraham's loss of justice or Tolstoy's loss of rationality. Like Abraham,
like Tolstoy, the scientist is now justified by faith
alone.

   The unification of space and time implies that
matter cannot be separated from motion; modern physics
visualizes matter as being in a continuous state of vi-
bration, a state of dance so to speak. The Hindu Shiva,
the Cosmic Dancer, god of creation and destruction, immediately comes to mind. And, quoting D. T. Suzuki,
Capra notes that like today's physicists, "Buddhists
have conceived an object as an event and not as a thing
or substance."[16] This idea forms another touchstone for
the parallels brought out by Capra. Again, it may be
said that there are no opposing forms but simply a variety of manifestations or movements of a primal oneness, a variety of interrelated events. In this connection Capra writes,

          Both the modern physicist and the
          Eastern mystic have realized that all
          phenomena in this world of change and
          transformation are dynamically inter-

> related. Hindus and Buddhists see this
> interrelation as a cosmic law, the law
> of <u>karma</u>. . . . Chinese philosophy, on
> the other hand, . . . has developed the
> notion of dynamic patterns which are
> continually formed and dissolved again
> in the cosmic flow of the <u>Tao</u>.[17]

The Chinese flow of the Tao may be compared to the Hindu manifestations of Brahman;[18] and for all the major Eastern schools of mysticism—Hindu, Taoist, Buddhist or Zen—the experience of transcending Oneness is the index of Enlightenment. The physicist's analogue is the unified field theory, the marriage of quantum and relativistic physics which would accomodate both the sub-atomic and the astrophysical scales.

By now the reader will have noted that throughout these remarks on the unity of interrelation there runs a thread of subjectivism. Here Eddington asserts, "All the laws of nature that are usually classed as fundamental can be foreseen wholly from epistemological considerations. They correspond to a priori knowledge, and are therefore wholly subjective."[19] Insofar as we are matter aware of itself, we are matter discovering its own physical laws, matter experiencing its own enlightenment as it were. In the words of Bohr, "we are both onlookers and actors in the great drama of existence," even in the drama of our own personal existence.[20] What we see is the way we see, and the way we see is what we are. In short, we see and experience ourselves—no more, no less. To be sure, one of the basic tenets of quantum and relativistic physics is that the frame of reference of the subjective observer is inseparable from his measurement of physical phenomena. Our perception of what is "out there" is shaped by what is happening "in here."

To the extent that consciousness seeks to objectify its world, it "is not the Self," as the Buddha phrases it, and "that is why consciousness is involved in sickness."[21] The soul who is before the world and not in the world is afflicted with avidya or "the wrong point of view" which results in futile grabbing at things; this in turn leads to duhka or suffering. In the <u>Gita</u> Krishna expresses it by saying, "One should lift up the self by the self, one should not let the self be degraded; for the Self alone is the friend of the self and the Self alone is the enemy of the self."[22] Speaking with the world as Thou engenders the relation that places the subject in the world; speaking of the

world as It generates the separation that places the
subject before the world.[23] The difficulty is to be
present.

Both physicists and mystics are attuned, therefore,
to the bond between the framework of subjectivity and
the articulation of truth; for all the differences between them, modern physics and Eastern mysticism find a
very important point of contact in the notion that
truth is subjectivity, to use Kierkegaard's phrase.
This is the bottom line of the parallels between the
two, but what about the metaphysics that brings us to
the bottom line, the metaphysics of subjectivity? This
is where existential philosophy may be of some help.

2

Metaphysics lies not so much in what we think as
in how we think. "Whenever we proceed from the known
into the unknown we may hope to understand," says Heisenberg, "but we may have to learn at the same time a
new meaning of the word 'understanding.'"[24] Modern
physics is a product of such a transformation of
thought, and it is this shift in the how of the physicist's thinking that has brought physics into conceptual contact with mysticism. The philosophical distinction involved in the movement from one manner of
thought to another is perhaps best described by Kierkegaard in his Concluding Unscientific Postscript, where
he explains the difference between objective and subjective thought:

> While objective thought is indifferent
> to the thinking subject and his exis-
> tence, the subjective thinker is as an
> existing individual essentially inter-
> ested in his own thinking, existing as
> he does in his thought. His thinking
> has therefore a different type of re-
> flection, namely the reflection of in-
> wardness. . . . While objective thought
> translates everything into results, and
> helps all mankind to cheat, by copying
> these off and reciting them by rote,
> subjective thought puts everything into
> process and omits the result.[25]

On the existential view, truth cannot be chiseled into
a law of contradiction or syllogistic structure; the
stasis of the formula is anathema to truth. Truth is

here conceived as a state of dance suspended by faith over the abyss; it is in process, just as the existing subject is in process. Or better: the presence of the conscious, existing individual is precisely the process that constitutes truth. This is how we are to understand the notion that truth is subjectivity.

It is easy enough to see the philosophical relation between Kierkegaard's version of subjective thought and the Eastern mode of subjectivity; indeed, the truth or "authenticity" of the mystic's experience and existence is inseparable from his meditative thought and the passion of his faith. This is what lies behind Krishna's assertion that "man is made up of faith. Whatever faith a man has, that he is."[26]

The metaphysical connection with modern physics, however, may appear more tenuous at first glance. One asks, for example, whether or not the striving for the physical law, for the solution to the equation, amounts to translating everything into results. Yet, as we have seen, physicists no longer subscribe to the idea that one may objectively observe laws at work or equations being balanced "out there" in nature. Says Einstein, "As far as the laws of mathematics refer to reality, they are not certain; and as far as they are certain, they do not refer to reality."[27] The mathematical equation belies the truth of the matter by translating it into a result, a fixed and static certainty. For when truth becomes result it is objectified and degenerates into something else; truth is never that which is spoken but is rather the speaking itself. Thus the philosopher's claim that the scientist's manner of inquiry enables "what is to become what it is"[28] is echoed by the scientist himself: "We have to remember that what we observe is not nature in itself but nature exposed to our method of questioning."[29]

Where truth is conceived as subjectivity, there are no fundamental entities, no immutable laws, equations or principles. As Capra has pointed out, physicists have realized that the so-called laws they use to describe the universe are reflections of our conceptual map of reality and not of reality itself.[30] In voicing the metaphor that maps the world, the self voices not only the metaphor of its relation to the world but of its relation to itself. When the world is objectified into an It, the self too is so objectified and is lost to the stasis of the It; when the self speaks to the world as Thou, it returns to itself as a Thou. This brings us to a very important aspect of the metaphysics of subjectivity—the self's relation to itself.

Kierkegaard offers the following definition of the self:

> Man is spirit. But what is spirit?
> Spirit is the self. But what is the
> self? The self is a relation which re-
> lates itself to its own self, or it is
> that in the relation that the relation
> relates itself to its own self; the self
> is not the relation but that the relation
> relates itself to its own self. Man is
> a synthesis of the infinite and the fi-
> nite, of the temporal and the eternal,
> of freedom and necessity.[31]

In keeping with Eastern mysticism, the self is here viewed as an _event_; in keeping with modern physics, the self is here cast in terms of interrelations. Kierke-gaard's definition, however, may call for a word or two of explanation. In this instance the self is to be un-derstood as a movement which takes measure of itself in such a way that the measuring is a hearing.[32] The self grows, pulsates and becomes while gauging the how of its growth, pulsation and becoming. The self stands in relation to its yesterday, its today and its tomorrow, and the manner in which it takes stock of that relation is what defines the self; this is the relation relating itself to itself. In short, the self is the process of weighing its own process of becoming. Dasein's being, in the words of Heidegger, is an issue for Dasein.[33] That is, the "being there" of the self is a concern for the self, and, taken subjectively, the self "is there" to the extent that it is so concerned. It is only with-in such an interrelational context, the context of sub-jective existence relating itself to itself, that the question, "to be or not to be," can arise; only here, where the subjective "was," "am" and "shall be" are an issue, may time be thrown out of joint.

Einstein has taught us that temporal constructs are born of the relation between one frame of reference and another, yet the very possibility of such a theory of relativity is a reflection of the self's ability to move outside itself. In _Being and Nothingness_ Sartre claims that "temporality can only designate the mode of being for a being which is outside itself. Temporality must have the structure of selfhood."[34] The self is able to relate itself to itself by virtue of existing along the referential horizon of temporality, of "before" and "after." It is at the edge of such a horizon, where the abyss begins to yawn, that the existence of the self becomes an issue for itself. But, as Heidegger points out, "the concepts of the 'future,' 'past' and 'present' are initially generated out of an inauthentic understanding of time."[35] Kierkegaard likewise considers this a false conception of time,[36] false because it divides and objectifies time into a series of "nows" which we grope and grab for until we never live but only hope to live; such is precisely the Buddhist "wrong point of view" which results in suffering. This is what happens when the self struggles to cling to itself as a permanent, object-like entity and thus fails to gauge the moment at hand in the ever-changing process of becoming. The misunderstanding arises, in other words, when the individual comes to a halt, paralyzed by a preoccupation with the next day. And where there is dread of the morrow, there is no seizing the day.

Such an understanding of time reinforces an important metaphysical link between physics and Eastern mysticism. The conceptual determination of a space/time continuum on the part of physics is in perfect agreement with existential thought, as with Eastern mysticism, since it places the thinking subject beyond the division of past, present and future. To borrow a phrase from Kierkegaard, time is annulled.[37] The mystical experience of the Brahman or of the Tao is, in part, the experience of the spatio-temporal unity of being, and here too time is annulled. In such a vein Capra writes, "To get the right feeling for the relativistic world of particles, we must 'forget the lapse of time,' as Chuang Tzu says."[38]

If temporality places the self outside itself, spatiality produces a similar displacement. One may find an expression of the spatial displacement of the self in Heidegger's Being and Time: "Dasein understands its Here from the viewpoint of its environmental There. . . . In accordance with its spatiality, Dasein is never in the first instance here but is rather there, from which it returns to its Here."[39] In the first instance I am instilled with the codes and the expectations of the people and environment around me, "out there." I am cast in the mold of a Man-selbst or They-self; contoured to the system of Das Man or the They, I know just where I fit in. Thus I see as They see and speak as They demand.

So it is that the self initially receives it existential accent and arrives at its autonomous Here when it finds itself lost "out there." The self first becomes conscious of its subjective existence when it no longer knows who it is or where it fits in. The temporal expression of such a problematic is "What will become of me?" The spatial expression is "Where do I go from here?" The spatio-temporal expression is the question "Who"—or better—"How am I?" Since none of these questions can ever be answered once and for all, something always remains hidden or veiled, and the fabric of the veil is the spatio-temporal framework in which we are isolated, our frame of reference. As the physicists have said, we can only perceive slices of the continuum. But according to the mystic, we may transcend the isolation of the slice in a movement of faith and experience the oneness of the continuum, thus penetrating the "not here, not now" of the veil. Inasmuch as the veil silhouettes the trace of nothingness, nothingness emerges as the source of the Not. "Dasein means being projected into Nothingness," as Heidegger puts it.[40] Indeed, such is the transcendence that restores the subject to the sum of what is. Kierkegaard too borders on the language of the mystic when he identifies the instant with eternity; the Kierkegaardian image of the instant "not as an atom of time but an atom of eternity"[41] suggests that within the instant one may move beyond the limits of space and time.

So far we have had a taste of the metaphysics of subjectivity as it pertains to the self's relation to itself. Let us now consider the self-to-world relation. If the existing subject "is there" in a spatio-temporal sense, his being there or Dasein implies being with or Mitsein. One observer always exists in relation to another; a frame of reference stands within a network of frames of reference. The structure of that network "toward which Dasein directs itself," says Heidegger, "is what makes up the worldhood of the world."[42] And in the light of the Not born of nothingness, being with means being within in the sense of standing in a relation to something or someone else, who is not I.

We have spoken of the self in terms of a relation relating itself to itself, in terms of a process. In that the world is a structured network of individuals standing in relation to each other, it too is a process. Moreover, our relation to another individual as other lies in the divisions and displacements that make us other to ourselves. In the language of Buber, "I become

I by way of Thou; becoming I, I say Thou."[43] Like the self, the world and the other constitute an event, a process of interrelational rising and falling, with the conscious self as the ever-changing yet autonomous point of departure and point of return. To use the quantum metaphor, the self is both the fixed, particle-like point and the dynamic, wave-like movement of departure and return.

At the end of his discourse on modern physics and its description of the world Capra writes, "Quantum theory has made it clear that these phenomena can only be understood as links in a chain of processes, the end of which lies in the consciousness of the human observer."[44] Kierkegaard's concept of truth again comes to mind, the notion that truth is subjectivity. This accent on subjectivity characterizes a qualitative vision of existence. Here the one is more than the many, for this is the domain of the spirit or the heart. Says Heidegger,

> The inner and invisible domain of the
> heart is not only more inward than the
> interior that belongs to calculating
> representation, and therefore more in-
> visible; it also extends further than
> does the realm of merely producible ob-
> jects. Only in the invisible innermost
> of the heart is man inclined toward what
> there is for him to love.[45]

The calculating representation mentioned by Heidegger refers to the quantitative, statistical dimension of life turned over to the crowd, where the inner life of the single individual is deemed at best unreal, at worst harmful. Thus, as Sartre has noted, outwardness establishes numerical quantity,[46] which in turn places the existing subject on a market of exchange. That is, whenever an individual must determine his identity along the spectrum of statistics, he must come under the look or regard of others, and this puts him in a position of negotiation. The movement of faith, the outcry of the spirit, is here cast aside, since such a thing is of no marketable value; the subject is transformed into an object. Das Man's insistence on ubiquity, stasis and conformity allows no room, no space, for the aberrations of subjectivity.

Such is precisely the focal point of Heidegger's concern for the relation between the individual and the

They, a concern which is indeed central to all philosophers of this ilk. By now one can see that just as the
individual may lose himself to the crowd whenever he
allows the crowd to speak his existence, so too may the
physicist lose himself to universal laws whenever he
allows the laws to speak his vision of the world. And
when the physicist has lost himself to the accepted
formula, he loses the ability to see and to speak the
truth. Examples of this in the history of science are
legion, and every scientific leap of the imagination
has been a leap of faith achieved by the insertion of
subjectivity, by the outcry of a voice that is speaking
rather than spoken. Thus we discover a vital aspect of
the metaphysics of subjectivity, namely that it is a
metaphysics of speaking.

"Because the They presents all judgement and deci-
sion as its own," Heidegger writes, "it deprives the
individual Dasein of responsibility."[47] The They speaks
the existence of the particular subject by paralyzing
his voice; the They eclipses the Word that calls for
response by its insistence on having the last word.
Once we have lost the ability to respond, to be re-
sponse-able, we lose the ability to hear. The inward
dialogue is drowned out in a choral mimicry. The many
absorbs the one, and the worst of all crimes is isolation, failure to join in. And so the lamentation of
Nietzsche's Zarathustra: "'All isolation is guilt!'—
thus speaks the herd."[48] Hindus describe the state of
paralysis induced by the prominence of the many as falling under the spell of maya and becoming chained to the
objectifying cause-and-effect of karma.[49] As the Buddhists might put it, the person who is locked into the
vision of the crowd is trapped in the vicious circle
of suffering known as samsara.[50]

Hence under the metaphysics of speaking there inevitably comes a point for physicist, philosopher and
mystic alike where the "crowd is untruth," as Kierkegaard says.[51] The difficulty lies in creating a language of the self, a responding which is at the same
time a hearing. In order to make the critical advance,
in order to become, the self must speak toward itself
rather than away from itself. And then it must respond
and listen to its response. The division of self im-
plied by spatiality and temporality may now assume a
sharper focus, since we can now see a connection between speaking and the process of becoming. The division of inward diologue is the separation—and the
union—of listener and speaker, the distance created by

the Word. For the Word implies process; the Word is not in time—time is in the Word. It creates and closes the gaps of sound and silence, of presence and absence. The physicist, philosopher or mystic may speak the metaphor of what existence is like, but the speaking that closes one distance only opens another; the gap reappears and beckons. In short, there is no set truth waiting to be expressed; there is only the struggle to voice it. Or better: the struggle is itself the truth. Thus the pulsating field is the only reality; there is only the flow of the Tao, the dance of Shiva. The subject is the truth, the dancer the dance, the voice the metaphor it voices. Truth is subjectivity.

If there should be something disturbing about this notion of truth, it is for good reason. If truth is subjectivity, then truth lies in the ability to make the movement of faith, and the self that cannot make such a movement is a counterfeit. This is what lies behind Abraham's fear and trembling; this is what generates the terror felt by the physicist when causality begins to collapse. Indeed, where truth is subjectivity all groundwork collapses, all handrails fall apart, whether they be reason, morality or causality.

In this essay I have brought out a few of the dimensions of the metaphysics of subjectivity which may add substance to the parallels between modern physics and Eastern mysticism pointed out by Capra. We have seen that at the heart of Capra's observations lies the idea that for physicist and mystic alike, the existing subject's articulation of reality helps what is to become what it is; that such articulation constitutes a dynamic interrelation between the individual and his world; and that such an interrelational process says as much about the subject as the reality he voices. The purpose of introducing a metaphysics of subjectivity was to bring out the how that inheres in the dance of the observer's relation to the observed. To do this, I first sketched the basic aspects of subjective thought and then examined the self-to-self and self-to-world relations engendered by such thought. Thus in pointing out a metaphysics than spans modern physics and Eastern mysticism, we have seen how an existential philosophy of subjectivity might provide the missing link that has frustrated critics such as Fowler.

In addition, we have noted a connection between the how of thought and the how of speaking: the metaphysics of subjectivity involves a metaphysics of

speaking. We establish a relationship with the world—
which itself makes the world a world—by giving voice
to that relationship; and this song is the existing
self. The process of self speaking itself, then, is
what we must bear in mind when the physicist speaks of
the gap between formula and phenomenon; when the philosopher speaks of a division of self and its distance
from the world; and when the mystic speaks as little as
possible, knowing that this reinforces the division—
witness the silence of the Buddha when asked about the
existence of the Self.[52] All three seek the proper silence and the language that is the peal of silence. For
all three have understood that "the significance of an
existential thought does not lie so much in its content
as such, as in what is happening to me in the thinking
of it."[53]

## NOTES

1. See Fritjof Capra, The Tao of Physics (Boulder:
Shambhala, 1975), p. 18.
2. Dean R. Fowler, review of The Tao of Physics by
Fritjof Capra, Zygon, 12 (1977), 266.
3. Arthur Eddington, The Philosophy of Physical
Science (New York: MacMillan, 1939), p. 111.
4. Capra, Tao, p. 68.
5. J. Robert Oppenheimer, Science and the Common
Understanding (New York: Simon & Schuster, 1966), p. 40.
6. Niels Bohr, Atomic Theory and the Description
of Nature (Cambridge: Cambridge University Press, 1934),
pp. 56-57.
7. Ibid., p. 11.
8. Capra, Tao, p. 135.
9. The Bhagavad Gita, tr. Eliot Deutsch (New York:
Holt, Rinehart & Winston, 1968), p. 110.
10. Capra, Tao, p. 211 (cf. Gita, p. 107).
11. Ibid., pp. 222-223.
12. The Upanishads, tr. Swami Prabhavananda and
Frederick Manchester (New York: New American Library,
1948), p. 56.
13. Gita, p. 83.
14. Oppenheimer, Science, p. 47.
15. Ibid., p. 35.
16. Capra, Tao, p. 270.
17. Ibid., p. 278.
18. See Gita, p. 109.
19. Eddington, Philosophy, p. 57.
20. Bohr, Atomic, p. 119.
21. Some Sayings of the Buddha According to the
Pali Canon, tr. F. L. Woodward (London: Oxford Univer-

146

sity Press, 1973), p. 21.

22. Gita, pp. 65-66 (see also pp. 44-45).

23. Cf. Martin Buber, Ich und Du in Werke, Vol. 1 (Munich: Kösel, 1962), p. 120.

24. Werner Heisenberg, Physics and Philosophy (New York: Harper, 1958), p. 201.

25. Soren Kierkegaard, Concluding Unscientific Postscript, tr. David F. Swenson and Walter Lowrie (Princeton: Princeton University Press, 1941), pp. 67-68.

26. Gita, p. 125.

27. Quoted in P. A. Schlipp, Albert Einstein: Philosopher-Scientist (New York: Harper, 1959), p. 250.

28. Martin Heidegger, "Was ist Metaphysik?" in Wegmarken (Frankfurt a. M.: Vittorio Klostermann, 1967), p. 3.

29. Heisenberg, Physics, p. 58.

30. Capra, Tao, p. 287.

31. Kierkegaard, The Sickness unto Death, tr. Walter Lowrie (Princeton: Princeton University Press, 1974), p. 146.

32. Cf. Heidegger, ". . . dichterisch wohnt der Mensch. . .," Akzente, Zeitschrift für Dichtung, No. 1 (1954), 66.

33. Heidegger, Sein und Zeit, 2nd Ed. (Tübingen: Max Niemeyer, 1929), p. 12.

34. Jean-Paul Sartre, L'Être et le néant (Paris: Gallimard, 1943), p. 182.

35. Heidegger, Sein, p. 326.

36. See Kierkegaard, The Concept of Dread, tr. Walter Lowrie (Princeton: Princeton University Press, 1944), pp. 76-77.

37. Ibid., p. 77.

38. Capra, Tao, p. 185.

39. Heidegger, Sein, pp. 107-108.

40. Heidegger, "Metaphysik," p. 12.

41. Kierkegaard, Dread, p. 79.

42. Heidegger, Sein, p. 86.

43. Buber, Ich, p. 85.

44. Capra, Tao, p. 300.

45. Heidegger, "What Are Poets For?" in Poetry, Language, Thought, tr. Albert Hofstadter (New York: Harper, 1971), pp. 127-128.

46. Sartre, L'Être, p. 44.

47. Heidegger, Sein, p. 127.

48. Friedrich Nietzsche, Also sprach Zarathustra in Werke, Vol. 1 (Munich: Carl Hanser, 1967), p. 585.

49. Cf. Capra, Tao, p. 88.

50. Ibid., p. 95.

51. Kierkegaard, The Point of View for My Work as

an Author, tr. Walter Lowrie (New York: Harper, 1962), p. 110.

52. See Some Sayings of the Buddha, p. 149.

53. Karl Jaspers, Vernunft und Existenz (Bremen: Johs. Storm, 1941), p. 95.